Maine Mediums
Mystics
and Healers

Maine Mediums
Mystics
and Healers

A resource of profound wisdom
for your life's journey

Cathy Cook

Brown Bear Spirit Publishing

Brown Bear Spirit Publishing

ISBN: 979-8-9881335-0-6

Edited by Mary Ellen Tracy
Cover photograph by Cathy Cook
Photographs of persons interviewed provided by the interviewee
Andrea Goodman Photograph by Rose Beverly
Book and cover design by Clif Graves of Hinterlandspress.com

Dedicated to:

All Mediums, Mystics, and Healers

Contents

We are not earthly beings having a spiritual experience; we are spiritual beings having a human experience.

— Teilhard de Chardin—

Introduction

I am excited to share with you my fascinating interviews with the following Maine Mediums, Mystics, and Healers.

Each extraordinary person I was blessed to meet shared unique insights and amazing wisdom. It was a joy and honor to meet these special, gifted people. Our conversations touched on several of the endless spiritual topics including how energy works, information about the afterlife, past lives, animal communication, numerology, astrology, medical intuition, astral travel, Akashic records, Reiki, and several other healing modalities.

Understand that we as souls are all gifted, we all are intuitive, and we are all healers. May you enjoy the stories, expand your thoughts, and receive knowledge and healing as you read the following pages.

Chapter 1

Denise Correll - Evidential Medium
Clair Extraordinaire

A friend, whom I once referred to Denise for an intuitive reading, told me afterwards that her reading helped her more than twenty years of psychotherapy ever could. I agree with her sentiment wholeheartedly and have received healing from Denise's readings myself many times over the years.

Denise is an extraordinary intuitive who guides her clients, through the messages which come through from their guides and loved ones in spirit, with compassion and understanding. For me, compassion is a quality which makes Denise stand out as a medium, as well as her strong connection to the spirit world, and the specific, "spot on" messages she gives. Denise is one of the best medium clairvoyants I know. I usually invite her over once every summer to give individual readings to friends on my porch, and these friends look forward to it every year.

Whenever I see Denise, it is usually for a personal reading, so it was all the more fascinating to hear about her background and abilities during the following interview. Denise is not only a very empathic medium and clairvoyant, she also has other intuitive senses: clairsentience, clairaudience, and claircognizance.

She has worked to refine her abilities with several well-known mediums and teachers, while working very hard as an evidential medium to be sure of, not just the validity of the message she brings forth, but to verify who the message is coming from, in her very articulate way.

Before Denise embraced mediumship full time, she enjoyed her other calling as a special education teacher and is also a devoted mother to her two sons who are now adults. These callings illustrate her strong, maternal and philosophical nature. She has degrees in Special Education: Emotional Disturbance/ Education K-12 and obtained her master's degree in Educational Leadership. The articulate insights on her website are clear evidence of her wisdom and talent.

I am a regular listener to Enlighted Empaths, a podcast Denise, and another gifted medium, Samantha Fey, have created. I have gained so much insight, wisdom and validation from their very engaging conversations and their interviews with other healers and gifted people. I have listened to them for so long now that they feel like close friends whom I visit often.

The following interview gives you some insights into who Denise is and some of her personal story:

I am very lucky that I grew up in a house where spiritualism was normalized. My father, who has now passed, was an incredible medium, empath, and intuitive psychic. However, if you go back to that time frame it was not something that he would go out and talk about with friends while he hung out at the wharf or the body shop. He was a very kind, hardworking, good guy and an incredible medium who was very connected to spirit. So, genetically I have that link. My mother was also highly intuitive and sensitive. Between the two of them, I grew up thinking this was a normalized environment and that was such a beautiful gift for me in my growing up years. But, as I grew older, I recognized that this wasn't everybody else's reality, and through different circumstances in my life I began to shut 'it' down. I was very blessed to grow up in a supportive environment, and also blessed to have the genetic lineage on both sides of my family of highly intuitive, sensitive people.

I believe most people have some semblance of either clairvoyance, or clairaudience. Some people start with

    Maine Mediums, Mystics and Healers

clairsentience, which is having clear feelings and the ability of sensing things about people, and then they often develop claircognizance, which is the sense of just knowing things even if you may not be sure why you do. I have found that over the years, you might start with one specific intuitive strength; however, the more that you do this work, and the more that you acknowledge it, the other 'clairs' come into play.

I've always been very clairsentient (feeling) and clairvoyant (seeing). Over the years the clairaudience (hearing) and the clairgustance (sense of smell) has also come into play. The beauty of this is that there is never a bottom; it's an endless rabbit-hole. You can never learn everything there is to know, and you can never become the best because there isn't a best. I love that about this work.

I've studied with many people including John Holland, Janet Nohavoc, Tony Stockwell, Colin Bates, and Lynn Probert, and I also did mediumship training at Temple Heights many years ago. I try extremely hard to take the ego out of the equation when doing a reading for someone. Part of my prayer and meditation before I do any reading is, *please let me get out of the way and let the message come through me and not from me. I don't want it to be about me.*

I believe most children sense Spirit, as they come into this world wide open. However, because of culture, social norms, or familial patterns, that sensing often becomes shut down. I think it's because you go from sensing being a normal thing, to it being a little unsettling. Often people say, "You can't talk about that, it's not real," or, "You are making this up." When I was very young, I saw what I believe was an angelic presence and I told my mother about it, describing a beautiful white light that I saw. She said, "Denise, there's nothing there. You couldn't have seen anything."

I must have been four or five years old, but I was so sure that I had seen something, and that image has been with me my whole life. I grew up very Catholic and I don't know if that was uncomfortable for my mother from a Catholicism point of view, or because I brought in an angelic presence. I don't know. I think the best we can do for children is to validate what they're seeing or sensing, so that they will not shut it off and think that they just made it up in their heads.

Speaking of children's natural experiences, I asked Denise something that I have become curious about. I asked her if she believed in the magical realm of fairies.

I think that it's multidimensional and there are so many possibilities. A good example is if you have done any shamanic work, (I had some training with shamanism as well) and you go into the woods, you can feel that higher energy. People who are plant empaths and people who are animal empaths, for example, are highly sensitive to the higher frequencies. If you think about the science behind it, everything is energy. Everything vibrates at a certain frequency. So then why couldn't there be multiple realms of existence? I thought about this as an intuitive or psychic; how do we tap into what's coming up? Is it already happening on another realm of existence and we're just picking up on it? That really might sound "wingnut" to some people, but that's what fascinates me; that there must be something there, for there is such a strong link for so many people. These stories could be traced back to all the Indigenous cultures. Magical realms have been around as long as there has been documented history. It's fascinating.

I asked Denise if she could explain how she experiences the messages that come through when she does readings.

When I do readings as a medium, I am using clairvoyance. I can explain it this way: You know how you can close your eyes and visualize a place; for instance, your childhood bedroom? In your mind you can go up the stairs and you know where the bed is, you know what color the curtains are, and you know where the books are, and so on. Whatever it might be, you see it all in your mind's eye. When I do a reading, I get a quick millisecond flash of a mannerism of someone; how old or young, male or female? I think, for example, do they feel like a grandfather? A lot of times to get the height of someone, I will ask the person I'm talking with how tall they are and for some bizarre reason it helps me determine the height of the person in Spirit and validates what is coming through to me. Sometimes I'll get the cause of death, because I physically get the feeling or reaction of how someone passed.

I have studied evidential mediumship because I want to

          Maine Mediums, Mystics and Healers

sense enough things to prove that I am on the right track with the person in spirit that someone is trying to connect with. If it's too general and there's not enough evidence to say that we're really making a link to the other side, it doesn't feel it is being of service to the person in Spirit or the person here who still loves them. You want to get a strong picture and you want to feel their energy. You don't want to just say, "Oh, it's your grandmother and she loves you," which is lovely, but you want to get enough evidence to prove that we're making a link to the other side.

Last fall when I did a trance mediumship class workshop, I learned to get to the point where you can invite a spirit to step into your energy, so you can feel their energy and their mannerisms. It is an extremely interesting experience to do that blend of energies with someone in spirit.

To explain how clairaudience works; sometimes I'll hear a song, or a foreign accent or I may even hear if they've spoken English as a second language. However, it is not their voice I hear. Clairaudience is your own voice in your own head, but it's instantaneous. It all happens at once. Again, I do the prayer and meditation, and I ask for the highest and best and to get me (my ego) out of the way. I'm more of a channel. I'm a channeling medium.

I have heard you talk about your observation about there being a shift in people's energy these days. Can you speak to the collective consciousness and what you think is happening with people in the world now?

It absolutely fascinates me, and I have started to document a little bit about this idea of tapping into collective consciousness. A few days ago, I spoke with a woman in Saskatchewan who is also a medium. She is in a different age group, different demographic, and different part of the world, but we were experiencing, almost verbatim, the exact same things in our lives right now emotionally, and spiritually. We're tapping into the psyche, and the emotional or empathic phenomenon that we're all going through as a people, and what I've found is the woman in Saskatchewan, the man in Albuquerque, and the person in Greece I talked to, are all having the same experience and tapping into something that's bigger than all of us. I believe the patterns that come through from that are very, very interesting. An example would be that before this Coronavirus pandemic, a lot of people were feeling fear and anxiety, and doom and gloom. They were having a sense that they wanted to make the most of their time left on the planet and were feeling like they needed to find more truth in their lives. Was that a precursor to this virus? Why are we all tapping into that, person after person? Why are all these people having the same experience?

About a year and a half ago, I used my phone as an alarm, but my phone went off by itself at 4 o'clock in the morning. I woke up and all of a sudden, I was downloading all this information and I started writing. It was pretty dense and heavy and uncomfortable information, but it ended on a note that we are getting ready to come into a time of peace and unity that we have never experienced on this planet before. It's about releasing these old paradigms and shifts so that we can bring in this new energy of healing. I believe that.

My other thoughts have been about how we are all interconnected and the earth couldn't do it anymore, and it's as if the earth said, *I need a break. I need to heal.* Because everything that is happening globally is happening as a society, and as a global society, we are all being forced by the Coronavirus pandemic to take a rest and let things heal. Mediums and empaths and highly sensitive people have been very selective about the news and what they are allowing in for information right now. It is so important.

What impressed me was that I was reading something online about a woman from Wuhan, and she was outside and heard birds and looked up in the sky, and she couldn't remember the last time the sky was blue! Think about how pollution has lessened everywhere as seen on the satellite cameras. In Los Angeles the sunsets are beautiful because of the smog, but everything was put on hold during the pandemic, and now the sky is clearing. This goes back to the collective. Just prior to this virus, we saw a young girl named Greta speaking to the world asking for a change, saying, *we need to shut things down- stop the engines- stop the world*, in order to save the earth from the devastation of climate change. Everyone was getting on board, there were parades and rallies and news conferences. Then suddenly, the world stopped because of the world pandemic. It makes me wonder, is that part of the collective consciousness putting the energy out there and manifesting it? It's interesting to think about.

I think that the polarity between light and dark is getting stronger and what interests me is that this virus completely mirrors the polarity of the present political situation. It completely mirrors the climate issues which also mirror the economic outlook of the "haves and have nots." It has been light against dark. Then the virus has been the first thing to affect us universally.

There is a sacredness to holding space for people who are experiencing grief. As a medium, I am humbled and honored to be a part of someone's healing journey. Being able to connect with those in Spirit and bring their essence back even for a few minutes is an amazing experience but with that there is a responsibility to hold space with as much love and compassion as possible. For me, this is service work and I am eternally grateful to be a messenger for Spirit.

In addition to personal and group readings, Denise offers mediumship classes for all, from beginner to advanced, and teaches Intuitive Tarot classes.

Information about how to set up an appointment is on her website, where she also shares her incredible wisdom and insights about spirituality: thegratefulmessenger.com. Be sure to also find her outstanding podcast with Samantha Fey, Enlightened Empaths, on all major podcast venues. You will be hooked!

Chapter 2

Phyllis Kenney - Tabletipologist

Phyllis Kenney describes Table Tipping as the favorite of her energetic healing modalities. Very humble and light-spirited, Phyllis's website, Connecting-For the Luvin Fun of It, lists her unique offerings, which include everything from table tipping, soul entrainments, spirit readings, past life regressions, aroma touch Reiki sessions, to awareness workshops, spirit groups, and crafts sessions. Phyllis is trained in hypnosis, soul entrainment, Reiki, and IET.

Time disappeared during the following interview, and two hours felt like twenty minutes. In Phyllis' own words:

Table tipping is the physical manifestation of spirit. Similar to the physical movement of a Ouija board, Spirit taps the table one time for yes, and two times for no. There is a potential for the table to walk itself around the room, but I have been doing this for so long that I no longer want to chase it! Sometimes the table will pivot on one leg and I have seen it happen that the top of the table has leaned down just inches from the floor, and then pulls itself back up. What I love about it is the physical phenomenon, it's difficult to dispute the movement when you "know" the answer and the table responds to validate your intuition. This is a great way for people to learn that everybody has an intuition, and everybody can tap into that higher source. If I tell them something from Spirit, they hear me and can easily dismiss it for one reason or another, but when they ask a question and the table moves in response, it's a whole different reaction. I've seen so many people just light up with excitement! That's why it's my favorite.

I have been told several times that the way I do table tipping is different from most people. When I do it, I give people a message from Spirit, and then we go into questions that the client brings forward. The second half of the reading is the table itself responding to client questions. Other people who do table tipping usually have the table respond with a yes or no to questions, but you don't get information prior. Just like with mediums or any other modality, every practitioner is different because every person is different. I have a friend who, whenever she begins a reading, she rubs her hands together, and I probably have my own quirks, but I don't know what they are because I close my eyes all the time while I am reading, so I am in a zone and not paying attention to myself. I try to get out of the way and let Spirit work through me. Letting go of ego gives the best readings! I tell folks when they come to do a workshop with me, that if a person you're receiving information from, either from a class or a session, doesn't resonate with you, it's not for you. Not every person's teachings or guidance is for you. Be discerning, but also be open. If you are closed off, it can make it harder for the medium to be in flow. It's an exchange of energies, the more you are open, the better and more fun your session will be.

A bit ago, I was doing readings with a group of friends, and I was down to reading the last lady and when it came time to ask questions, I said to her, "You've got something that you need to share tonight."

She had a funny look on her face, she started to deny it when her friend said, "You're not...?" She said,

"Yes! I am pregnant!" So, sometimes things just come out during a reading that you didn't mean to let out! Sometimes I'm as surprised as my clients about what comes forward! I always ask for the truth as Spirit knows it at that moment. Things can change, circumstances can change, etc. We have free will, thank goodness, so we can change!

Table tipping is just lovely, and I enjoy it when people have that 'ah-ha' moment. It's great for clarification for something that you have been pondering and can't seem to get out of your ego to get answers. That's the beauty of it, asking for help and receiving it. (Sigh), everyone should experience it with a good practitioner. If you do go and you didn't enjoy it, please try another spirit reader, you'll be glad you did.

Each time I do spirit readings or work with the table, I work with my teachers, guides, and angels to bring forward your teachers, guides, and angels. I ask that healing take place and that you receive information that is for your highest good and that it be the truth as they know it today. I also ask for something you want and something that you need. That's my prayer every time, and sometimes it changes a bit depending on the situation and client. A practitioner should be working with the highest source. I also share that whenever you are going to a reader, healer, car dealer, doctor's office, grocery store, etc. that you ALWAYS surround yourself with divine white light. Allow your angels to protect you and keep you. You can do this for your loved ones and for folks you know who might use an extra prayer today. I also ask for this divine light to encompass folks who are unsure how to ask for it. Your guidance is here to help; just ask.

Often, during the reading, I give the person information on who is working with them currently in Spirit, and that's the energy that will be answering with the table. It's most often NOT who they "want" to come through. We do get to ask if the person they are looking for is with them and sometimes you'll feel a shift in the energy and know that that person has stepped forward to answer questions. Clients around the table can often feel the shift and sometimes the air temp will change too, again physical shifting. Very cool. Sometimes the person they are looking for is not there or not willing to step forward. I explain that it's not like I have a direct line or just hollering to the neighbor next door.

My guidance tends to bring information for folks to help them with forward movement. It's what I look for when getting a reading. I look for confirmation on my next step or maybe I am looking for what I'm supposed to focus on next. I think my guidance tends to do this for other folks as well. It's nice to get confirmation through the table on steps you take to shift and change, or to bring in something new such as a relationship or business and know that this is the best move for this moment in time.

I do workshops, but I don't claim any of the titles. One of my favorite things to do is called Soul Entrainment®. It is a version of hypnosis, which I am certified in. The way this works is that I put you under hypnosis and I talk directly to your soul. It is incredibly profound, and I am blown away by it every single time about what comes forward in a session.

I asked Phyllis if the soul is the same thing as the higher self, and Phyllis said she believed that it is.

The Soul Entrainment® is profound, because I am speaking directly to the soul and the soul responds. The information which comes forward is just incredible. Initially when I took my training and I experienced it personally in a session, I was shocked and amazed by what the response was to the questions asked. The ego is gone, and the answers are from the purest, highest levels of your awareness. It's incredible. I don't do enough of them. Everyone who has experienced it so far has had the same response I had - feeling a bit stunned and humbled. There has been uncontrollable laughter and most often many tears. You feel lighter and yet a bit fragile by going so deep. It's a must do.

As a certified hypnotist I also offer past life regression sessions. I was facilitating a group past life regression session a couple years ago, and as it turned out, each client had brought a friend along and there were three sets of friends. Everybody was on the floor getting comfortable. I took them through a series of meditations and hypnosis, and I asked them to work on something that is happening at this time that they want information on. Then we went through a process of regressing back to a past life as we were in the group session, and then we came back together. I asked everybody to write down their information, and then I asked if they wanted to share with the group. One woman began to share her story about what she saw, where she was, what she was feeling, why she was there, and what she got back as a tool for this lifetime. A woman across the room was just sitting there with her mouth wide open, and she said, "I wrote almost the same thing. I think I was there with you at that farm!"

She brought up a lot of the same information that the other woman had experienced. She said, "I think we were there together."

As the facilitator, it's absolutely phenomenal to witness and be a part of the healing process.

I can tell you an experience from a personal past life regression. When I was training to do this, I was the 'guinea pig' one night in a group session. There were friends who knew me there, and the facilitator had me under hypnosis. I was a Native American male in this life, and I kept thinking, *how could this be?* The facilitator kept talking and was prompting me, but you're in it, and the voice of someone talking is distracting to you. He was bugging me, like a fly, and I kept shooing him away. The facilitator asked me my age and I said that I was in my fifties, and I knew that my hair was white. I looked like my grandmother, my skin was so wrinkled, and I thought, *how can that be*? I felt so old, but I was only in my fifties. I was sitting on top of a bluff, and I was looking down watching soldiers. I knew this was the end for us, and that we were not going to make it when they showed up. She asked me what I learned and what I wanted to bring back to this lifetime, and I said, "I am proud."

Oh my gosh, I tell you that was incredible! In the other two life events that she took me to that night, I learned more important truths. *I am alone. I am proud. I can do it.* I was a cave person at that moment, and I almost hit her! I almost punched the facilitator in the nose because she was bugging me, and under hypnosis, in my mind, I was trying to hand her food. I had my hand out and when she brought me back, the whole room was trying not to laugh out loud!

When I came out of the hypnosis, everything I had experienced was so vivid in my mind. The emotion that comes with it is incredible. So, when you get to experience it, you get to share it. That is why it is another of my favorite things to do, and I love it.

I asked Phyllis at this point if she thinks that we are all old souls, and I was surprised that she said we are not.

I believe that some souls come here as new souls. They are the ones who can't get enough information, and they have to experience absolutely everything. They have no fear whatsoever. They want to touch everything on your desk, and they don't even know that they are doing it! What they are doing is collecting all of the data, because they don't know if they're going to be coming back here again. They just think they are going to do it all. I also believe that a young soul can have ancient wisdom, but the soul is young and they want to experience everything. The billionaire who owns Virgin Airlines is an example of a young soul, I believe. He's the one who's trying to put people into space. He got out of structured schooling and was voracious in his quest for knowledge, He shouldn't be where he is today, but he has to experience everything. Young souls are like gatherers, and they just have to know everything.

The old souls are the ones who are cautious about everything, like my granddaughter, who thinks like, I've been here and done that, so I don't have to jump into that puddle because I know there's mud in there and I don't want to get my boots wet! They just look at you with these eyes and they don't get rattled. Those are old souls, and they're coming back to experience something, but they are not the ones with the hang gliders, for example, they're going to do everything in a way that is safe.

I asked where all the new souls are coming from, because I had always thought that we've all been here before many, many lifetimes.

Energy is born constantly. For me, I believe we belong to soul groups or clusters, and the way I see it is that these groups of souls are like a bunch of grapes. That's why someone can be your soulmate, without having to be intimate with them. It can be your best friend, who knows you inside and out, and who knows when to call you or who finishes your sentences. I hear people say, "I thought we were soul mates, but we're breaking up." I tell them they may be in the soul cluster, but it doesn't mean they have to be attached to them. It might just mean that they are here to learn something from the other person. New souls are being born constantly because energy is always being recreated.

I tell people when they come to my workshops that you are not going to learn any new knowledge from me because I don't have any. What I can do is teach from my experiences. I am a hands-on learner and that's how I work. When I do a workshop, it will be Spirit driven. I used to try to create down to the opening and closing prayers, but I'd put all of that detail in, and my guidance would go in a different direction based on the clients who were there. If am doing a workshop on using pendulums, I may spend the first fifteen minutes working on an issue you bring forward, so it's organic, and that's now my preference. I like giving a message to a participant because that's what Spirit wanted me to do.

Do you do this work full time?

My day job is working as an administrative assistant. I am an introvert working on being an extrovert, so being in public is not an easy thing for me. Not so long ago, you may only have heard of me through whispers. My friends were just sharing the stories of how they came to meet me. "Hey, I have this friend, I think you'd like to meet her." They'd be invited to a table tipping night that I was having at my home. We were laughing about when my friend called to ask me to do psychic dinners and I shocked BOTH of us by saying yes. She said she couldn't believe it! So, I do this a few nights a week. I know other practitioners that go to homes, but I did that and had some not-so-great experiences, so I don't do that often.

When I was a teenager, back in the day, anything metaphysical was considered "occult," and it scared the heck out of me. I have a cousin who is four years older than I, and she was always dragging me to all kinds of places. One of the first people that she brought me to was Mrs. Albert on Green Street in Augusta, and that was my first experience with physical manifestation. Mrs. Albert was in her late 80s at the time, and I was around age fourteen, and she had a chair that she would have you sit in and then she would sit across from you. Her spirit guide was a little Native American girl named Lily, and this little girl would knock on your chair once for yes, twice for no, and when she knocked, you could feel it! I was so scared and so intrigued, I don't even remember my reading, but I do remember her telling me that she would astral travel, and also, she described to me what my dad was doing at that moment. She said that every single night he would get up from the dinner table, make a peanut butter sandwich, and go watch the news. When the news was over, he would light a cigar and fall asleep. She's telling me this, and my eyes were just like dinner plates and my mouth wide open! The chair was banging underneath me, and she was telling me exactly what my father did every night! I was so petrified, but she was absolutely amazing. If I had known then what I know now.

The Augusta Spiritualist Church, for me, was like going home. I felt like I found my tribe, and these were my people. I was in my 20s when I started going there and I was so intrigued, and I couldn't get enough of it. Later when my kids were older and I was divorced, I began going to Thursday night classes at the Spiritualist Church. I found out then from my mother that her grandmother read tea leaves. I thought that would've been nice to know, back when I was a kid and I thought that I was weird for what I was feeling and seeing. Family has such an influence on your thoughts and beliefs. I was so scared based on family, but my soul was so intrigued, I needed to know more! My mother had a lot of fear that she unknowingly passed on to me. When I became more involved in working with Spirit, she tried to get me to stop. So, one night she decided to come to table tipping with me to see what it was all about. She decided that it was okay, but she didn't want to do it again.

I believe everyone has this capability, but I also think it's about whatever you want to put your energy into, and where you put your focus. I would love to be able to sew, like my sister who makes beautiful quilts, but I just wasn't interested in spending that much time doing it. I would rather spend time playing with my pendulum or better yet a table! I just think it's just like anything, some people are concert pianists, and then there are other people who put all kinds of time into something else. Table tipping and soul work are my absolute favorite things to do and they are so profound, truly. I just love doing this spirit work.

A few months after my phone interview with Phyllis, I met her in person at her friend Bonnie's house to experience table tipping. If you could hear the recording I made on the ride home recounting it, you would understand how amazed I was. I kept saying over and over, "Wow. That was cool!"

I really liked Phyllis immediately, as she is so upbeat and bubbly! As I sat at the table, I felt all tingly with energy and it made me think of when I was a teenager and the only medicine for seasonal allergies at that time was Sudafed, which made me all buzzy. I could feel the hair on my head. I have had many readings over the years but never felt the energy like that before.

Phyllis began the session by instructing us to lay our hands lightly on top of the small table, and as soon as Phyllis began her opening prayer, the table began to move around slightly. I admit I was trying to be inconspicuous as I watched Phyllis's hands and glanced down under the table a few times to see if she was somehow making the table move. Bonnie's spirit guides came through with a message for her first, and I was amazed at the action of the table and how it moved around. Very soon I just accepted it as a reality, and it seemed natural.

When it was my turn, the table actually came right up against me. It was a hug, Phyllis explained, from an old friend. When she said this person was someone who charmed me, and that most people didn't 'get' her, but that I did, I immediately knew. "Is it Charlotte?"

Phyllis, or actually the table, said an emphatic yes, with a big tipping motion! The table continued to respond to my yes and no questions, with emphasis at certain times. As my messages from Charlotte came forth, I just thought how physical and real the whole experience was. Charlotte, an elderly lady who I had become friends with years ago, and who had since passed, said that I had a big celebration coming up next summer. Charlotte told me, through Phyllis, that she wanted to help me with anything I wanted help with. She added that she and I were connected, and that we shared a love affair of the heart. I was so happy to hear from her, and was moved to tears. Phyllis said that Charlotte was my "Girl Friday," and that all I have to do is ask, and that she will help me.

Phyllis had told me to come with questions that day, and the only question to ask that I could think of on the ride over was, who my spirit guide was! Table tipping with Phyllis and Bonnie was so much fun and very moving as well. I absolutely loved it.

You can contact Phyllis at her website: *https://www.tabletipologist.com*

Chapter 3

Francine Hicks - Psychic Medium, Gallery Readings

I met Francine several years ago when I was invited by my friend Nan to a gallery reading. Francine is a medium clairvoyant who can connect with people's loved ones who have passed and bring messages forward. During a gallery reading, she sits within the group, closes her eyes, and begins connecting with the spirits of their loved ones. She can be very specific in details, and she has a great sense of humor, making it a fun experience. Since that time, I have invited Francine over to my home many times to do gallery readings with a group of close friends whom I have known most of my life.

It is very interesting to watch how messages come through, when being a part of a group reading. Francine says she usually sees people in spirit on the other side lined up and waiting their turn to speak to their loved ones. The spirits often stand behind the person they came to speak to.

One interesting, memorable night as my girlfriends and I sat in the living room with Francine, she said to me, "Do you know you have a man in the kitchen?"

"That's just Rick doing the dishes," I said. (He was probably trying to stay out of the way of us women gathered in the living room!)

Francine laughed and said, "I know, but there's a man standing behind him. It's his father, and he is saying something about a car."

I called Rick into the living room and Francine told Rick that his father stated he was trying to help him when he works on a particular vehicle in the garage. Rick is a car mechanic and radiator repairman who specializes in old classic cars. Francine said Rick's father wanted him to look at the idle air control, (or something close to that). Rick was stunned and said he had been perplexed with what was wrong with the car. Rick was working on his father's 1971 Jaguar in the garage at the time. Rick nodded with disbelief and said, "That makes sense," when Francine related the detailed message. Francine did not know that Rick was a mechanic and worked on cars.

Francine also told Rick that his grandfather was present as well, and that he spoke in some kind of foreign language which Francine had never heard before. Rick was impressed with Francine's intuitiveness as his grandfather was Armenian. Rick's grandfather Henry had come to the United States in 1919 to escape the Armenian genocide which had wiped out much of his family. The grandfather said he was one of Rick's guides, and stated it was a very easy assignment because Rick was such a good man, and on the right track in his life. So true.

Francine always brought forth messages about the ghosts and spirits at our home, an old inn once called the Androscoggin House, in Wayne. Former guests of the inn loved it here so much that they still visit occasionally and sometimes watch over the place. Francine more than once has seen a couple she thought were caretakers, and she described the man as very tall and wearing old-fashioned clothes and a top hat. For some reason she always saw them on the stairway. Every time she came, she also saw a woman upstairs, who was always sweeping the floor with a broom. The last time she was here, Francine sensed the woman was trying to keep the energy upstairs separate from the downstairs. Other mediums who have visited here have described seeing a woman sweeping as well. Interesting. There was for a long time a vortex in a certain place in the hallway upstairs, and some funky energy there, we were told, by other visiting mediums. Perhaps it was the funky energy that the woman was trying to sweep away?

Francine was as much fun to interview about her mediumship as she is during gallery readings. She likes to tell stories to illustrate how she believes the spiritual world works.

The questions I hear the most are, what happens to my loved ones and what happens to people when they die? Did they have pain, and did they suffer? Normally, when I talk to someone in spirit they don't come out and just say, hey I had a heart attack, and give the specific cause of death. Instead, I feel what happened to them when they died. If it was a heart attack, I feel pain in my chest. When I connect with someone who has passed with a lung disease, I find it hard to breathe or have heaviness in my chest. I might feel pain in my head if someone has had a stroke, and so on. I learned to interpret what I was feeling was their way of giving me information. But the message most people get is that their loved ones have no more pain, and are at peace where they are.

Sometimes when people cross over to the other side, they still have issues to work on, so they are not fully there yet, and they cannot be reached. Sometimes if they are having trouble adjusting or just need to complete the transition, they cannot be reached. Eventually they are able to connect to this world. (It takes a while before the spirit can come forth and speak to their loved one). For example, my father didn't come through for a very, very long time. He was an alcoholic and he had a rough childhood, so he had his own personal issues to work on, I believe. But after some time had passed, my sister couldn't go within five feet of a medium without my dad coming through! She was his favorite.

Francine, can you speak a little about what you think it's like on the other side and what our loved ones are doing?

From what I have seen on the other side, it is peaceful and whatever the person wants it to be. I've seen people fishing all day, baking, planting flowers, and doing anything that they truly loved to do in this world. It is whatever their heaven would be. Think of a place with no worries or concerns and you could spend your time doing whatever makes you the happiest. I know that our loved ones watch over us. Sometimes that little voice in our head could be them giving advice or warnings. I know that they want the best for us and sometimes they are best able to help us from above.

Speaking about mediumship, I think everybody has the gift if they want to explore it, but not everyone wants to do this. I know that my sister could become a medium if she wanted to, and I know that one of my nieces is very in tune with it, so to speak. This niece doesn't explore her gift very much, but one time after going to a channeling class together, she had an interesting experience. As we walked out onto the street, a bus went by, and she had a really strange look on her face. I said, "What is the matter?" She asked me if I saw anyone on the bus. It was around nine o'clock at night and only the driver was on the bus. But it wasn't really empty, there was a young person who had passed on the bus.

I said, "Oh, did you see that young lady in the third row from the back?" My niece gasped,

"Oh my gosh, was that a dead person?" I replied, "Yes it was." It was kind of frightening for her and she said,

"Now I see what you mean about how you see them, but you don't really see them."

I explained it's like they're not fully solid, if you will. I love the movie "Ghost," because the way ghosts are portrayed is how the ghosts truly are. Not everyone wants to do this. It can be exhausting for most people. For me it is energizing.

For me spirits and ghosts feel different. The ghosts almost feel like they are still here, whereas people who have crossed over feel completely different. It's as if the ghosts don't have that feeling of closure about them, and it doesn't feel like they moved on. When I see ghosts, they feel stuck to me. Maybe they just like to hang out, or maybe they don't know that they can move on. For whatever reason they stay here in this realm sometimes. The ghosts look different than those that have passed. They have a more solid appearance. Our loved ones who have passed are very transparent. I can see what is around them and what they are seeing. With ghosts, it's not like that.

I started the channeling class about twenty years ago. I don't like the word "channeling." I learned from a woman named

Judy Garbow who is a wonderful teacher, Reiki Master and IET Healer. My first class was more about automatic writing, which is where you sit still and meditate, and thoughts come into your head and you write them down. It's a way of connecting to Spirit. I grew up Catholic, so it was hard for me at first, and I had to work to get away from the old belief that mediums are practicing witchcraft or dark arts. It made me nervous, but I watched Judy as she channeled the ascended Masters and other teachers, and her voice would change and her whole body and posture looked different. I asked her, "Doesn't that freak you out because someone else is coming into your body?" She said no that it's actually very nice.

One day I said to myself, fine, I'm going to just do this. Judy suggested I should channel someone I trust and I said, "Okay, then it has to be Archangel Michael." I don't know why but I have always thought he is one bad ass Angel. If you want any angel on your side, it should be Archangel Michael. I love him. So, Judy told me she was going to put Archangel Michael into my body. The feeling was unbelievable. His energy was amazing. She warned me at first that the energy was going to feel intense. Immediately, I felt like my whole body was huge, and I felt like my head was on fire. I had an incredible peace. I began to talk with Michael and other ascended masters. I was able to see Jesus. When she brought me out of it and everybody else in the class was talking amongst themselves and then, boom, there was a dead person in the room that I could see. I just stared at him. It happened that quickly. It was the thing I needed to be open. Judy said she thought that I just needed to let go. Allowing Archangel Michael to enter my body, allowed me to open to Spirit.

A lot of people in the class knew each other. There was a girl who talked to the class about her cat who acted crazy and ran back and forth with his ball, which flew across the room by itself, and the TV went off and then it would come back on. I looked over at her as she's going on about how crazy her house was and I blurted out, "Do you have a brother with blonde hair about eighteen years old?"

She said, "Yes, why?"

"Because he's right behind you!" She immediately started crying. Her aunt who was with her said her brother had just passed away a few months ago.

The girl was astounded, and I told her that her brother was telling me that he was doing all that stuff with the cat and the ball and the TV because he wanted her to know that he was there with her. That was the very first time I connected that way with Spirit.

The earliest thing I remember years ago when I was young, was that I used to get woken up in the middle of the night with what seemed like a hundred voices in my head. It was just maddening. I would just lay there and think, stop, stop, just please stop. After a while it stopped, and I never heard another voice. When I brought that up to Judy, she said, "You know, you were clairaudience originally, but you made it stop." She told me that if that ever happened again, I should say, please, one voice at a time, and please slow down.

After the channeling class, I began to see and feel things everywhere I went. At first, I thought, gosh, I'm losing my mind, but now I know that I was actually seeing and feeling Spirit, and it makes sense to me now.

I believe everyone has intuitive feelings which come out when they go someplace or they are about to do something, and they have this inner feeling that says, don't do this, or I don't like that place, or I don't want to go there. Sometimes people feel a strong dislike or distrust about someone they have just met, or they just have that "knowing." That's why you hear people say trust your feelings or trust your gut. We all have a pretty good built-in guidance system if we pay attention to it.

I was so honored when Judy started calling me once in a while and she would ask, "Hey can you give me a reading because I don't know what's going on with this person?" I was so honored. She told me that this is my special thing; that I am a medium.

Judy is also a wonderful animal communicator and some of my favorite stories which she would tell about, were of her talking with animals. I thought, I love how animals talk to her. I am a cat show judge in my spare time, and I also show dogs. Occasionally I'd ask her, "Hey, what is wrong with this dog (or cat) today? He's making me crazy!" Eventually I learned that I could communicate with animals too.

Once, after one of our cats had passed away, I said to my husband Mike, "Did you see that? Petunia just ran down the hall -what is she doing?" He was stunned at first. Our animals who have passed come back to visit us and I find it very comforting. When I see a cat in spirit, it's not quite solid, but it's not like I can see through it either. I don't know how to explain it, but it takes space. It's very interesting.

One night my husband and I were sitting in the living room and I said out loud, "Right down the hallway. Go visit them." My husband looked at me, puzzled. Our friend who was a cat breeder had just passed away. He had a lot of cats and they ended up with me because I was helping him find placement for them before he died. I said, "Oh for God's sake, they're right down the hall there, the door on the left." My husband said, "What on earth are you talking about?" I said, "It was just Richard; he's looking for his cats." I do that to people a lot, apparently, and especially to my husband, and then I say, "Oh I'm sorry, I forget that you can't see these things!"

Francine, can you speak here about what is the difference, if any, between channeling Spirit and mediumship? Under what circumstances do you channel? Is that what you are doing during the readings?

I don't think there is a difference. Maybe the difference is who you are channeling? I channel when I am asked or when I am looking for some information. Other than that, I just let them tell me what I need to know. Channeling covers mediumship for sure. You must connect to Spirit in order to do this. The information comes in different ways, depending on the person. I can see and hear and feel and sometimes there is just a "knowing." All of these are forms of channel. They're just so real to me that I forget other people can't see them.

Talking with animals really cracks me up. As a cat show judge, I get to talk to a lot of cats. There are some breeds of cats that talk to you, and they never shut up, no matter how much you tell them to! There was once a Siamese cat that was driving me crazy. Judy and I laugh about it together, how much the cats at the shows talk all at once. In the beginning I wasn't conscious that I was talking to them, but now I am able to comfort them, and tell them they need to cooperate. It definitely helps to be able to communicate with them.

Sometimes people bring me the cat that is most difficult to handle, because they know I can work with them. Some of the cat judges say, "Oh Francine, you are like a cat whisperer!" Of course, I do not tell them I can communicate with them. If they only knew! Sometimes the problem is that the cats just don't want to be there. One lady said to me "We promised our cat that if she attained the highest title, we wouldn't make her do the shows anymore. But once she got the title, we figured, oh we will just finish out the year with her. But the cat got worse and worse every show." I said, "Well apparently she didn't like you lying to her!" Obviously, the cat got mad when the owner didn't fulfill the promise. This cat was just a maniac, but had never been a problem before. It's just about developing an understanding of the cat." Some cats do not like the shows. Cats try to do their best and they want to make their humans happy.

The dogs at the dog shows don't really talk to me so much. They are more business. I think that's what makes me sad at the dog shows, is that they are so over-trained. It's almost like they trained the personality out of them. My new dog, Bella came here from England, (as a generous gift, she is my late dog Ozzy's sister.) Bella is a show dog and my husband and I laugh all the time because the dog is very British and stands very still and allows you to pet her. She looks at you like, oh please! She's a very proper little dog, but you see little glimpses of a crazy, fun puppy too. She is spoiled and can do anything she wants.

Giving the readings helps people a lot, and that's what I love about this. I do both gallery readings and one-on-one readings, as well as readings over the phone. I don't advertise, I just think whoever needs me, will find me.

My brother-in-law, who has passed now, could see things too. He was a Reiki Master and very open spiritually. When my wonderful mother passed, we had an amazing experience. At her funeral, it was like heaven opened up and I was able to see it all happen! Everything was bright white, and I looked at my brother-in-law, and we both saw her ascend to heaven! It was absolutely amazing.

I also saw her spirit leave her body when she passed. Before she died, I told my mother that when people pass, they always have someone who comes to get them. I saw her dad come to get her, and her sister too. It was so interesting and beautiful the way it happened. I know people go to a better place where there is no suffering, but I also know it's hard to lose people we love.

After my mother passed, whenever I was in the car, she would be always in the car with me. She was always there. Sometimes, I thought, here I am, driving around talking to my dead mother! But suddenly it stopped, and she wasn't there any longer. I called Judy and said, "I don't know what's going on, but all the sudden my mother is gone, and I can't reach her." This was after she had been with me for months and everywhere I went constantly.

Judy told me I needed to move on. She said, "You're never going to heal from her passing, if she doesn't go away." That was hard for me. It forced me to let her go. This might be an interesting problem that mediums have when their loved ones pass away. Normally when you lose someone they're gone and you have to start that grieving process. But with my mother, she never left, and I could still hear her and talk to her. I believe people often have similar experiences with feeling the presence of a loved one, or seeing signs they are near, especially right after a death.

Not everyone knows that I am a medium. In fact, the majority of people in my life don't know about this. I wish that more people believed, because it is very comforting knowing that there is something waiting for us.

I have worked for many years as an assistant in a medical office, and one of my co-workers knows that I have "gifts" and it freaks her out a bit. She also knows that I can find missing items. For some reason finding things for her is very easy for me. The way she found out that I was a clairvoyant was when she lost her wedding ring and was very upset. She was devastated, looking everywhere in a panic. I felt bad for her and wanted to help. I asked her if she had a pool table, and she said yes. I asked her if there was someone home at her house and she answered that her son was home. I told her to call her son and tell him to go look in the far-left pocket of the pool table. She called him, and after a few minutes she came up to me in disbelief. She said, "You have never been to my house before. You didn't know I had a pool table. How on earth could you have known where my ring was?" I said, "Actually, your cat showed me where it was."

She just said, "What!?"

I thought, okay, the cat's out of the bag. Now she knows about me. I said, "That darn cat of yours sure likes your pretty jewelry, and he likes to move it to other places, doesn't he?"

Eyes wide, she nodded.

"Yes, he does!" I said,

"Well, he took it and put it in the pool table pocket!"

She's used to me now, and I helped her when her father passed away a few years ago. I was able to give her the date of her father's passing, which she appreciated, and it helped her. The time-thing is hard, but sometimes they (Spirit) give it to me. Sometimes they give me these dates that are vague, but with him, they gave me a very clear date. When it was time for him to go, she was more prepared. "You just know things," she always says to me. I say, "I know nothing; just what they want me to know!"

Some people find gallery readings challenging, but for me it's sometimes harder to do one-on-one readings. I think the pressure is off people when they are in a group, so they are more open and relaxed. Sometimes people are guarded during the reading. If something private comes up, I offer to talk more with them in another room. Most of the time, if they know each other well, they can help each other with the message if it doesn't make sense to them at the time. It's interesting for people to hear other people get their message and that "ah ha" moment, when they get something about a message that comes through. I don't know how many emails or phone calls I've had days after a reading, and they'll say, "Oh, I get it now!" It can be a little overwhelming and emotional, so people forget some pretty important things.

I'm lucky that people want to do the gallery readings because I really enjoy doing them, and I get so much energy from the experience. A lot of mediums say they feel drained after readings, but for me, I'm just bouncing off the walls! Physically I get tired, but spiritually and energetically, I am very energized. I think it is because when you're channeling spirit, the lightness attaches to you, and stays with you. I feel very thankful for my gift and the experiences I have.

For anyone who would like to set up a personal or gallery reading, I can be reached at: francinemhicks@gmail.com

Chapter 4

Kelly Dawn Purington -Evidential Medium

Coincidentally, I met Kelly at the town office where I work. I told her she made me think of a medium named Kelly who I had seen on a pamphlet which I had picked up at a psychic fair. I was interested in contacting her for an interview in the future. She said she was the Kelly Dawn Purington! We began talking and set up the following interview about her gifts and experiences. Kelly describes herself as an evidential medium and psychic. I felt her warmth and big heart the first time I met her. She lives at Camp Etna, a spiritualist camp in Etna, Maine.

All my life I have felt different from other people. I remember having a hard time in school, because I was always very sensitive and I had trouble focusing. I experienced a couple of tragedies when I was young which made me want to explore spiritual communication.

I lost my grandmother when I was ten years old, and I began having the most vivid dreams of just sitting on the steps with her and talking. I knew that she was coming through to me in the dreams and I knew it was her talking to me. It was very beautiful. Dream visitations are fairly common, because it's easier for our loved ones to come through when we're asleep. I had many conversations with her when I was a little girl. It was then that I became fascinated with spirit communication. I have always been sensitive to others' emotions, and I came to know as an adult that I am an empath.

My father was into spiritualism, and as I got older, I learned that he occasionally attended the spiritualist church in Augusta. I didn't find that out until later in life, but he was definitely an influence and inspiration to me. My father and I started experimenting with the Ouija board. Many people think negatively about the Ouija board, but it really is just a tool to communicate, and it's more about what you put into it. For me, I always had the intention to go into it with good energy. I started doing that with my father; I opened up more and more, and because of the tragedies that happened in my life, I started learning spiritual writing. I desperately wanted to communicate with the other side, and the communication that came through was pretty clear and accurate. I've always been someone who did readings for friends. As I got older and I had my children, I still was doing readings for my friends informally.

My practice with automatic writing gave me confirmation about people on the other side and the messages I got. My father told me he was going to see a local medium and I asked him to ask her about me and my gifts. The medium confirmed my abilities and said, "Tell her to make sure that she's all in."

The way I understand that now is that it is a different energy to be in, and it's a big responsibility to give people messages from Spirit. You want to take it seriously and you want to take very good care of yourself. It's not like a typical job, because working with energy is like being in a different reality. I always say to people that I try to be as far outside of my brain (ego) as I can be when I connect with the other side. A lot of mediums walk around open to Spirit all the time and they don't know how to close it down. You can protect yourself by having contracts with your spirit guides about boundaries; that you're not willing to get a message from Spirit at 3 o'clock in the morning when you're asleep, for example. It's important to be able to take care of yourself spiritually and to be in your conscious brain. But when you're doing a reading, you have to be able to switch over to utilize the gifts that you have, and to go into that energetic space to do a reading.

I've always been highly empathic, but I didn't realize until I was an adult what it really was. Right now, a loved one is experiencing that same thing, where he is very sensitive and feels what other people are feeling. I explained to him that if he gets to school and someone talks to him in a completely appropriate way, but he picks up on that person's strong emotion or anger that it could be about something that happened to the person back at home. It could be that person's stuff, not his. I tell him to stop and separate himself from it.

I do a lot of teaching, and I have a class called, "Observe but Not Absorb." Typically, people who do not understand being empathic can become filled with anxiety, because having all emotions come at them at once is difficult. Some become shut down. A person can become overwhelmed if they are very empathic and not protecting their energy field. So, if a person is feeling an emotion that doesn't match anything that's going on with them, or they are feeling particularly fearful or feeling any other deep emotions, they should say to their spirit guides, "If it's not mine, please take it away."

You might have to say it a couple of times, but it will disconnect you from that other person. For example, I have a dear friend I worked with, and I was very connected to her. One day I was having a panic attack and I thought to myself, *there's nothing in my life causing this.* Within minutes, the phone rang. It was my friend who was working out in the field, and she said, "Kelly, I am sitting on the side of the road, and I am having a panic attack."

I knew at that moment it was me connecting in, but again, going back to my childhood, I was always like that, and I thought it was something wrong with me. Empathic people also tend to need a lot of time alone, and even as a child, I used to wander off into the woods, and go off by myself a lot. One of the techniques that I use is to ask my spirit guides to take it away. When I'm doing readings, it's the same thing. I have to connect into what someone is feeling to do a good reading for them, but I also can't be affected to the point where I can't do the reading. I ask my guides to lift it.

I've learned over the years how to work on protecting my energy field. There was a period of time during which every time I went out in public, I came home wiped out. Another thing to be aware of is that the more sensitive you are, the more you pick up on what's in the collective consciousness. It gets deeper than that. There are processes you can do, and there's not just one way to do it.

I would recommend taking a class on how to use being empathic, rather than it using you. The process of learning this requires me tapping into your energy and seeing how empathic you are, whether you are simply picking up on other people's emotions who are near you, or if you are tapping into a situation or someone not present in your vibration. Other factors are that you may be picking up on physical pain as well as emotional. My class is called "Observe, Not Absorb."

I believe we have different spirit guides at different times in our lives because we need different levels of support and guidance for what we are going through. In my experience I've had a couple of guides who have been with me for quite a while, and as we need them, they show up. I tell people all the time, if we are listening, we will be guided to what we need in our lives. We are always led to where we are supposed to go if we just pay attention. It is very interesting.

My guides are like my gatekeepers, and I believe that we all have different spirit guides throughout our lifetimes. I don't want to walk around my house open all day long, so I have a ritual to open up and then my guides know that I want to open up, and they assist me. Also, I have a steadfast rule that I do not predict death, so my guides know not to give me that information. I don't think it's ethical to tell someone about an impending death. Also, if I knew someone was going to die, I would feel obligated to try to do something to prevent it. My guides help set the rules for an accurate reading that it is in the best interest of the person being read. I believe a person's guides come through with messages to help them for their highest best.

Mediumship is very interesting because when Spirit communicates with you, it is like a cell phone connection, sometimes the information is loud and clear, and sometimes it comes through broken up and you have to piece it together. My guides also show me visual things using my memory bank, in the form of symbolism. I am always interpreting what is being shown before giving it to the person I am sitting with. It's an interesting art.

Evidential mediumship means I do my best to validate that you are talking to the person that you want to talk to, or the person who is coming through, by giving specific information. When I give a reading, I feel the person in spirit more than I see them, so I may describe them more by their personality, as opposed to describing them by physical appearance, like how tall they are. I do, however, get very specific information visually as well. For example, I was doing a reading for a woman, and we were bringing through her grandfather, and he showed me what looked to me like a sword. He showed me a leather case for it, and then he also showed me a ring with it. If I were to think about it, I would have been confused. I said to the person, "This is what I'm seeing, a sword and a ring in a leather case." After the reading, when she got home, she texted me a picture, literally, of a miniature sword and a ring together in a box, which belonged to her grandfather. I have never seen anything like it before, but that is what I saw exactly.

That's an example of evidential mediumship. It could be as simple as a specific description of how they looked, or a pair of boots that they owned. Evidential mediumship is important too and supported by the spiritualist religion. Rather than saying, "I see your grandmother behind you and she loves you," I want to give more specific information that has substance.

I am a member of the Augusta Spiritualist Church, and a member of Camp Etna, where I currently live. We have our own camp church service during the summertime when our summer programs open up, and there are Camp Etna Mediums who serve the church. There is a different medium every week who leads the church service. Sometimes it is a Medium from Portland and sometimes a Medium from as far away as Europe. We have quite a variety of gifted people. There are only a few of us who actually live here all year round. Most people show up in the spring and stay through the summer. We have private cottages that people can rent, as well as auxiliary buildings with rooms. It is a special place.

One thing that people have come to know me for is that I am very quirky, and I tend to be very animated when I do a reading. I move my hands around a lot as my spirit guides often give me specific mannerisms to get the message across. Here's an example: I was doing a reading for a couple who had lost their son. The woman asked me if their late son watches over his young daughter. I said yes, but my hands became cupped together and I found myself holding them in front of me. This is my cue to pay attention because I'm not moving as I normally do, and it was a weird sensation, because not only were they utilizing my hand movements, but they were also utilizing the feel, and I can feel things pretty intensely. I felt like I was holding someone's bottom in my hands! (Laughter.) And I'm getting this weird look on my face, and it turned into a life size teddy bear, and I'm holding it in my mind. As I was acting this out, I told them that he showed me a huge teddy bear. At the end of the reading, she showed me a picture of a teddy bear that would have been bigger than the child, and it was something that she did not have when her son was on the earth plane. It was as if the son was saying that he knew his daughter had a great big teddy bear, and it validated he was watching over her at that time.

I'm quite a shy person normally, and if I went to a party where I didn't know many people, I would probably tend to be off in the corner keeping a low profile. However, my friends joke that if was doing mediumship, and a spirit came through that danced on a bar table, I would probably be up there dancing on the table! I've been known to use whatever I need to get the message across, and have it be accurate information for the person getting the reading.

I also do table tipping, and I love it because it is physical mediumship. It is probably as close to the Ouija board as anything, and I just enjoy doing it. It's a different way of communicating, where the spirit comes into the table to communicate, and it brings them closer, in my opinion. When I'm doing mental mediumship, it's a different connection because with table tipping, the person sitting at the table can feel their loved one. For instance, when you bring through someone's child in spirit, because you never forget the feel of your child, being able to feel that is important and powerful for the parent. Likewise, there is nothing better than a late pet coming through the table, and it can be so emotional. I used to work out of an office, and we offered special sessions called "Psychic Sample." Many people look at table tipping and are hesitant to try it. With the Psychic Sample, people had to pay for three different readings and would sometimes end up trying table tipping though it wasn't their first choice. Once, I had a couple who came in and the man looked at me and asked what the table tipping was about. I explained it to him, and the table started tipping and it immediately went right over and sat next to him. I could see his dog in spirit sitting beside him with his paw up in his lap. I'm explaining this to the man and tears start rolling down his face. He was not going to participate at first, but when he did, it was very meaningful for him.

I have a favorite table, but I've used even TV trays in a pinch. You can pretty much call the energy to any table, but I do have a favorite style as well. Some people like using a three-legged table, but mine is rectangular and on a pedestal with four legs. There's a woman named Joni Mayhem who is an author who writes ghost books, and she came, and she wrote an article about me, and also videotaped me doing it, and that's also out there.

I started offering psychic dinners a few years ago in local restaurants, and I go table to table offering readings to people as they dine. It is very fun. In order for everyone to get a message, I couldn't do it alone, so I eventually brought in other mediums who I trusted and knew their work. It has become very popular and is often sold out quickly.

I don't just do this to make a living; this work is my heart. It goes back to when I was a young teenager. I had lost a dear friend and I wanted desperately to connect with him. Now, I can be that connection for other people, and that means a lot to me, to be able to sit with people and help them, especially if it is with grieving the loss of a loved one. It can be gut wrenching to give these emotional readings, but at the same time I would never give it up, because I know from experience people need that help.

I can tell you a lot of stories, but what it all comes down to is that I love helping people. I am grateful for my gifts and being able to connect with Spirit and deliver healing messages.

To contact Kelly for a private reading, home mediumship party, or banquet, call 207-949-1154 or email mediumkellydawn@gmail.com.

Chapter 5

Judy Garbow-Spiritual Savant

My original interview with Judy was very fun and interesting, and I learned so much about the shift in energy that is happening now in the world, as well as about spiritual realms and channeling. Judy is an encyclopedia of spiritual knowledge. She was referred to me by Francine, another medium and friend who is featured in this book, and who became a channeling medium after studying with her. Judy is a very eclectic healer who emphasizes the need for each of us to grow and evolve into our own unique spiritual knowledge and beliefs and gifts. Judy studied for many years with spiritual teachers all over the world and is truly a spiritual savant. I learned about things I didn't know existed. I also learned about myself and received meaningful messages from Spirit from Judy. She gave me detailed insights about a troubling situation in my life as well as information about my own healing abilities.

Judy has a very contagious and joyful energy that is healing in itself. Judy sums up her energy work in the following way, emphasizing that she is always changing and growing:

M any years ago, one of my guides Tushwa, channeled
through my dear friend Jilly, gave me the title of Spiritual
Savant. My studies have taken me throughout my work
in the healing alternatives from Animal Communicator, Holistic
Nutrition, Angelic Channel and Medium, to teacher of the
Healing Arts, which is ever evolving for me. Healing is definitely
an art and the gift is recognizing that. Having spent years of
personal growth working with clients, I feel blessed to be able to
speak from experience during these ever-changing times.

Just the other day I was online looking at a video of a lawn
ornament when a song played from the video that did not fit
what I was looking at. It was Bob Dylan's Blowin' in the Wind.
The realization for me in this song was how much it fits our
current situation today. Some songs are timeless no matter
when they were written. As Tushwa said many years ago, "That
which is not coming from truth and integrity is coming up to
evolve." Our messages are constant if we just learn to listen and
trust our intuition. We are consciousness and we are constantly
being guided. All we need to do is ASK. We are all intuitive and it
is important to remember that and own it, or to re-learn what is
a continual gift that keeps on giving. We are in a time of
remembrance. Everything is vibrational including music, color,
and thought patterns. Our very busy minds give us a chance to
create or learn to quiet, feel and experience life. Our animal and
nature kingdom are the best teachers of living from the heart.
Those of us who choose to awaken have found them to be the
greatest teachers of unconditional love.

What I do is read energy. I share my gift in that way, but I
encourage you to find yourself in the information that comes
through me and through you. My goal for you as a client and for
us as a human race is to find ourselves in our energetic
experience. We create our own reality and thus we are able to
change it. How we react to the world and our own experiences
is personal. We are blessed at this time to be able to see the God/
Source/Universe in everyone and everything with a knowing of
what is right for us. We all have a path to take and mine started
when I was very young, but I did not recognize it until years
later.

I help people to discover themselves, improve their lives
and enhance the lives of their animals. Everyone has the

opportunity to re-open their natural gifts as we all open up in our own way. Trust in your differences; that is the way to become the gift of yourself.

Judy can be reached at her website: Seastar Organics.

Chapter 6

Linda Huitt - Holistic Practitioner and Teacher

Linda Anzelc Huitt is a Holistic Practitioner of several energy healing modalities. She is also a teacher, providing certification, training and enrichment workshops to her many students, and a coach, leading her clients to clarity and empowerment in their life. Her healing practice, Pathway Of Joy, is located in Buxton, Maine. Linda provides healing services which include Integrated Energy Therapy® (IET), Kundalini Reiki, Usui Reiki, Melchizedek Method healing, ThetaHealing®, Akashic Records readings, and Life Coaching. She also offers healing sessions and readings for pets. I met Linda at a holistic fair and she offered me a ninety-minute session of IET® healing. I myself am a level 2 Reiki Practitioner, and I have experienced Reiki healing, but the IET session was more powerful, emotional, and just plain magical than anything I had ever experienced before, for healing.

It was explained to me that IET is similar to Reiki healing as it is an Eastern-based energetic method, working with your chi (your lifeforce energy), but using a higher vibration. Like Reiki, IET sessions can be performed both hands-on in-person, and as "distant" healing sessions. The healing room was very relaxing with soft music playing and the subtle sound of a waterfall. After I laid down on a comfortable, warm massage table, I closed my eyes and was aware that Linda was moving her hands over me. She drew symbols and asked the nine Healing Angels, my spirit guides and my personal angels to come in to work with her to clear my energy centers, heal, and empower me. Linda placed her hands gently on me, beginning with the top of my head, and slowly moved down my body as she worked throughout the ninety-minute session. I could feel the energy through her warm hands and she gently explained which areas on my body she was clearing. As she did this, she described the images or phrases which came to her as she worked through my energy field. Each time she began to clear stuck energies, she suggested that I could release certain issues, fears, or emotions, if I wished to. It was very powerful, and at times emotional and I could feel tears falling down my cheeks. Though this may sound dramatic, I felt it was an important ninety minutes in my life, as I tried to focus on Linda's words and the healing energy I received.

Linda asked me before we started what issues I would like to address and I told her I would like to work on anxiety and self-esteem issues. The first symbol she saw during the session was a turnip, and she told me she heard the phrase, "I didn't just fall off the turnip truck." I immediately told her that I said that phrase all the time to my children, and she said my angels told me that I didn't need to say that to them any longer. (This was addressing my self-esteem issues, and I knew the angels knew that my teenaged children often had a way of making me feel stupid.)

The next thing she said was that she saw a coliseum with a bright light shining out of all the windows, and a lion in an arena. She sensed that the light was my soul shining and illuminating the windows. That really struck me, especially the part about the lion, as I had never told anyone this before, but I always wondered if my intense fear of lions was because I was once, in another lifetime, fed to the lions during Roman times. I know that sounds far-fetched to many who will read this, but it is true. Another interesting image Linda saw was that of a wolf paw, and she said she thought a wolf was giving me a "high five." That felt very good, and we later looked up the symbolic meaning of a wolf, and the meaning resonated with me. It was also suggested the wolf was one of my animal guides.

It was an absolutely powerful and amazing experience, and I planned to go back in a couple months for another healing session. I loved it. While I was lying there receiving healing, I kept thinking that I wanted everyone I know to have this experience. Linda told me that the healing might continue for days, even possibly weeks after the session, as the angels continued to heal me. I was aware that I truly felt lighter after my session. My experience was not dramatic, but it was very relaxing, and I loved every minute of it. It was as if I was mesmerized by what was happening during the session. I will add that even a couple weeks after, I noticed my gut issues had improved and that my whole core felt better, lighter, almost as if I had lost weight. It reminded me that when I had a Reiki session a few years ago, I thought my gut issues had been cured, and likely I was feeling the clearing of blockages in that area of my body.

The next night I had one of my recurring dreams in which I am usually back in my college years, and in the dream, I haven't been attending classes, and I do not remember where my classes are. I am stressed and too embarrassed to even ask for help, even if I could remember who my advisor was! In this dream, for the first time, a woman dressed in a blue suit sat down with me and was helping me find my schedule and classes. I was so relieved to be getting help. When I awoke from that dream, I wondered if the angels were continuing to help me heal from that anxiety on an unconscious level.

Linda, who also teaches IET, summarized it in this way:

Integrated Energy Therapy is an energy healing modality, and it is similar to Reiki in that we are working with your Chi or life force energy. IET came to be in the mid-80s and it was channeled to Stevan Thayer from Angel Ariel, so it is an angelic healing modality." She then paraphrased Stevan's story for me: "He was an engineer and he was going through a midlife crisis when he started learning about Reiki and practicing Reiki. He was working with a client one time and was having difficulty removing one of her energetic blocks. Then, he said he felt as if someone sneaked up behind him and all of a sudden, he was using techniques that he hadn't done before. He was feeling things and saying things that he didn't really know. He was completely aware of what he was doing, and he talked with the client about it and they agreed they liked the techniques, and they agreed to continue. Over time they actually wrote a book together, Interview with an Angel, with Stevan channeling Angel

Ariel, written by Stevan and his client Linda Sue Nathanson. (This book is available on Amazon and other book vendor sites.) Angel Ariel continued to bring him more and more techniques, which has now become the healing system that we call Integrated Energy Therapy®."

Linda went on to explain to me that some people think of Reiki as working with chakras, and depending on how a practitioner learned Reiki, they might or might not work with chakras, but most people are familiar with them. IET on the other hand works with a map of cellular memory, with nine main energy centers in the body. In each area, the practitioner works with you to release trauma, and then replace the trauma with empowerment energy. The empowerment integrates into your body to help you to shift to a more joyful, natural state of being. Everything is joy and compassion based with the support of healing angels. With any energy healing modality, it is best to always empower after clearing. A way to explain this might be to imagine if you go to the beach and you want to fill a hole in the sand with shells and make beautiful sculpture. If you dig a hole and walk away for a few hours the tide is going to refill the hole with water and sand. If there's something that you want to be in that hole, you need to fill it immediately. Another example might be if you dig a hole in your yard for a potted plant and you walk away for two weeks and then you come back, it will all be filled in. If you want something specific to be in there, you need to fill it immediately. So, with IET you receive a clearing and then you receive empowerment.

Not only is it a super high vibration energy, this method carries with it terminology that makes it fairly easy to explain healing to clients, so that they understand what type of trauma is being released, and what empowerment is being provided. Linda teaches four levels of IET certification training: Basic, Intermediate, Advanced, and Master-Instructor. Each level builds on the techniques and attunement energy of the prior. She also teaches IET® for Pets, helping her students to work with the non-human animals in their lives, and IET® for Kids, a certification training for children ages seven to 12.

Interestingly, Linda led a completely different professional life for about thirty years, working in the corporate world, before she had a personal experience which was the beginning of her career transition. This led her to her vocation as a holistic practi-

tioner and teacher. Linda had experienced chronic hip pain, and her doctor referred her to someone for stress management, and this doctor eventually introduced her to Deepak Chopra's teachings, which resonated deeply with her. Later, Linda received training in Reiki and other healing methods, and eventually made the change to becoming a Holistic Practitioner and Teacher. She opened her own business, Pathway Of Joy, in 2012, transitioning to it full time in 2014.

After my healing session, Linda talked with me and shared her wisdom about energy and spiritual concepts in ways I had never heard explained before, and she helped me to better understand energy, a hard concept for me to grasp. I especially liked the way she explained that we each have a "perfect, innocent soul wrapped in our human, ego-bodies."

I would like to share some more of Linda's wisdom and concepts.

"We all have both physical and nonphysical bodies, and we learn about the physical body all through school, and in high school we learn about our physical DNA. Our physical body is what you can see, touch, and feel; for example, when you pinch your skin, it hurts. That is your physical body, but if you take a little snippet of your skin, and put it under a super powerful microscope, all you will see will be the movement of molecules, and the movement of energy. Your physical body is where your energy is the densest and is the lowest vibration. As you start to move out away from your body, you get into the nonphysical, and as you move further and further away from your body, it is less dense. It is a higher vibration. There are layers to your energetic being. This can sometimes be seen in aura photos. Each individual has different and ever-changing colors in their aura, or energetic field, which are connected to different feelings, emotions, and beliefs."

Another fascinating concept Linda mentioned during my IET session, which I had never heard of before, was called the Soul Star energy center. She explained that the Soul Star is commonly thought of as the eighth chakra.

Linda also offers Akashic Record readings. She is an Advanced Certified Practitioner of Dr. Linda Howe's Pathway Prayer process, and went on to explain her beliefs and understanding as follows:

"The Soul Star, located a few feet above your head, is in the spiritual layer of your energy field; the spiritual layer is that part of you that coexists with the Divine. It's like your spiritual mailbox. It is where you put out your meditative energy or prayers and receive your answers. The Soul Star is where your Akashic Records reside. Your Akashic Records contain the vibrational record of your soul through all lifetimes – past, present, and future. It is the book of your soul and contains wisdom about your soul journey.

In an Akashic Record reading, we connect with your group of guides. Some of these energetic beings may be souls of people who you knew in this lifetime, and some might be more etheric or angelic and never had a physical body. Together, we connect with your guides to gain wisdom about questions you might have. Your questions could be about a decision that you may be trying to make. For example, one might ask, *Should I stay in Maine, or should I move to California?* The guides will explain what your life qualities are likely to be if you stay in Maine, or what it might be like if you move to California. They will not tell you the "right" answer because there is not a right answer. They will always honor your free will. They just give you an idea of what you may experience depending on what you choose to do. And since you have free will, if you don't like what is presented to you, you have the ability to make different choices to redirect your energy and life situation."

I asked Linda if the Akashic Records could be used to find out the source of an issue in life, such as the fear of speaking in public -- one of my fears. She explained:

"We can ask questions about how this fear is supporting you or serving you at this time, or what the purpose is of your relationship to this fear. Or we could ask to be shown a place and time where (Cathy) was very comfortable with speaking in public, was able to speak in front of thousands of people comfortably and was revered for that. We might be shown another lifetime of (Cathy's) soul. And then we might say, "please help us understand what shifted between that lifetime or that experience and the current lifetime. What happened that caused the shift to fear?' And a third part of that question might be, 'what wisdom can we take from that lifetime to help her in the here and now with releasing her fear of speaking in public?"

During my IET session at one point, Linda said she was releasing from my "karma points" and I asked her to explain what karma means. Her answer defining her belief in what karma is made sense to me.

"Karma is not about life getting even with you for being a bad person at some point. Karmic patterns are recurring patterns in your life which are here to help you have an experience or learn a lesson that you are meant to learn. It will show up in your life as recurring patterns of, for example, always being late, or always finding yourself in a situation where you are annoyed with the person you work with. For example, even after you changed jobs to avoid a person you were annoyed with, a new coworker may eventually exhibit some other similar behavior that annoys you like the last coworker. That is a karmic pattern, and the angels set the stage for you, thinking, oh she did not quite get her lesson when she moved from that job. Then they lovingly reset the stage, and maybe this time they might make it a more obvious or stronger lesson so that she can see it."

"I had a situation where I had a coworker who I got along with fine, but all the sudden she was very annoying to me. I wondered, *what is going on? Why is her behavior bothering me now?* I had an Akashic Record reading and what I learned was that my annoyance was like Spirit holding a mirror up to me. What I realized was that what was annoying me about this coworker, who suddenly was seemingly very controlling, was a mirror of my own tendencies to be controlling. Quite often when someone is bothering or annoying us, it is a reflection of ourselves. You can take the lesson and do what you want with it - you can shift your own behavior, or not shift your behavior. But if you at least have the awareness that this is the root of it, you can make your decisions."

If you would like to learn more about Linda Anzelc Huitt and her latest offerings of healing modalities, coaching services, and workshops, visit her website (www.PathwayOfJoy.com), or contact her at PathwayOfJoy1111@gmail.com or 207-329-7192.

Chapter 7

Nicky Allen - Psychic Medium

Nicky Allen is a gifted Psychic Medium, Hypnotist, Past Life Regression Therapist, and Reiki Healer, who also does distant work, private, and gallery readings. I met Nicky at a friend's home for a gallery reading with a few like-minded friends. Nicky's warmth and intuitive messages made for an enjoyable afternoon, watching how Spirit works, which is always fascinating to me. Nicky gave me accurate and detailed information that day that comforted me about worries that I had about a personal situation.

Later we talked on the phone and the following comes from our interesting recorded conversation:

I love working with Spirit in any way I can. One on one readings, gallery readings, virtual readings - all are wonderful ways to bring joy to people. It can be challenging doing gallery readings, especially when there are a lot of people who are related to each other and I have to separate who wants to speak with whom, and who the actual message is for. I have learned that the message that comes through is not for me to figure out because I am just a channel, and spirit works through me for the people that I'm sitting with. I have noticed that often the message fits more than one person there, and I think of it as if they are piggybacking on each other. When Spirit wants to come through, there are several people there, and time is limited, the spirits can bring forth messages that resonate with more than just one person. If you're working with a group of eight or ten people, and there are numerous spirits that want to come to each person, it can be a lot. What I have been shown is that spirits come in together when there are certain characteristics that resonate with more than one person. This happens especially with grandmothers for some reason. Hence, spirits jump in together and give information that sometimes fits two or three people. They tell me they all want a turn, and one spirit might be especially strong and wants to talk all the time because they are so excited to speak to their person. They want to talk, and talk! Sometimes, I have to go to them and say, "Hold on, everyone needs a turn here!"

As a medium, I do my best to make sure that everybody has the same amount of time in the circle. I can't control that all the time because Spirit is in charge, but I do ask them to give everybody something.

I want the people I'm working for to feel at peace after their messages; to feel hope and the love that those on the other side have for us. I do my best for everybody, and I want people to leave with a lighter heart. When I do my prayers before each reading or group, I always ask that the messages are of peace, hope, love and understanding. I am not there to bring doom and gloom, but messages of love.

Working with Spirit shows us that life is continuous - that our soul lives forever. I've been shown that we are all able to communicate with Spirit in some way. Just like any other gift, we all have varying abilities.

Around the year 2000 I had been through a very severe break up, and a friend took me to my first reading with a medium, and it hooked me! After that, I began attending a Spiritualist church and there I started my real training as a medium. I took mediumship courses and I started working the platform at the church. Eventually, I started doing readings on my own.

I asked Nicky if there were any indications of her spiritual gifts as a child.

I saw Spirit quite a few times and often it was through dreams, or what felt like dreams. It is funny because, though there have been a lot of negative things that happened to me in my life, I have always felt very lucky and very fortunate. For example, something bad would happen but good would come out of it. I could see this happening.

My maternal grandmother was a strong Catholic woman from Canada, and my mother and her siblings went to a convent for schooling, but I remember noticing while growing up that my grandmother was always talking to someone. My grandfather died before I was born, and I always wondered if it was him. She couldn't speak English. I do speak French, but it's limited so I never had a good conversation with her about her beliefs. Did she see Spirit? Did she believe in life after death? She died in 1986 and though she comes to me often now, I wish I had been able to discuss everything with her.

The first time that I remember seeing Spirit was in my grandmother's home. I lived with Memere for a while as a young teen because in my family there were four of us girls in a small apartment. She lived downstairs from us and had a spare bedroom that we redecorated for me. There was an elderly woman who boarded there with Memere in the 60's, maybe 70's, who had passed. I remember waking up and the woman was sitting in a rocking chair making one of her braided rugs, right beside my bed! I was pretty scared as I was only about thirteen years old.

I also had a few episodes where I woke up at night, and I knew that Jesus was in my room. Most of my experiences were just a "knowing." For instance, I would be driving somewhere, and I would feel like I needed to go a different direction, and then I'd find out that there was an accident on that other route. If I had continued the way I was going, I would have been in an accident. My knowing is sometimes like a prodding, telling me to go here today or to go another way. I found out one time that a boyfriend was cheating on me. When my son had a bad toothache, and I didn't have any medicine in the house, I had to go out to a store in the middle of the night. I had to drive by my boyfriend's house and I saw that he was gone at midnight. I realized that it was Spirit's way of letting me know what was going on with that boyfriend. That's the way Spirit works for me sometimes.

The 1820 farmhouse that we live in is haunted. I remember the day that we came to look at it, and as we were leaving, I looked up and there was a little boy in the bedroom window. I thought, *oh interesting!* Other people have also seen spirits here, and I have had instances of incredible assistance from the spirit I call "the farmer man." I believe the spirits here visit from time to time because they like it here - they're not "earthbound," as they've crossed over, but they like to visit their old home. The first part of this house was built in 1820 and the original barn was built around 1850. This place was a dairy farm until 1950, but until we came here, there hadn't been any animals for many years.

We had an old barn and we used to have llamas, goats, rabbits, chickens, and geese. It was a lot of work, and my husband had to travel a lot for his job. We had a lot of animal chores, and one time I walked down to the barn at night and went into the feed area. As I walked down the middle aisle of the barn, I looked down at the stalls and I thought *okay, this one needs water, and that one needs water.* I went to get the food first, and when I came back, all the water buckets were out of the stalls sitting in the aisle! I was stunned, and looked around thinking, *who is here?* I could smell cow manure which is how I've always known when the farmer man was around. I guess he knew I needed help that night!

I was curious if Nicky could pick up on any spirits in my house in Wayne, as I also live in an old house, and many visiting friends who are sensitive sometimes pick up on spirits and ghosts here.

There is a female vibration that is extremely strong there, and I want to say that she was there from the beginning, and she is showing herself to me in a long blue dress. It's not a fancy dress, but it was her best dress, so I don't think they had a lot of money. She keeps talking about someone named Mary, who's younger than her and who she takes care of. I am thinking it was her child, but she has her on the same level, so I think it is her sister or a cousin. She is showing me a bloodline, so it is someone related to her. If you haven't found out about her yet, you will.

The woman is telling me that *not all of us got buried in a cemetery or even with a marker or a stone.* I think she was though, and Mary would be buried somewhere around her. I had the distinct feeling that there are people buried on your land when she told me that not everyone is buried in a cemetery.

There is also a lot of native energy on your property as well as fairy energy. Of course, fairies are the guardians of the plants and the gardens, and it makes them happy when we honor plants by growing them and helping out our pollinator friends. So, make sure you have some good pollinator friendly plants there. There's definitely fairy energy there, oh my gosh. You yourself have a big connection with the elementals; you are connected that way. I believe in them myself. There's a reason why those fairytales have been written.

Another medium who I talked to a month earlier said some of the same things to me; that this property is very old and that it has strong native energy, and the other medium even mentioned people buried on the property. Very interesting!

Back to our conversation about mediumship, I asked Nicky if she believed that people only get messages from their guides that are helpful and in their best interest.

Guides always have our best interests at heart. They are with us to assist us in our "travels" here on the earth plane. Guides are often spirits that have not walked the earth plane. Many times, ascended masters come through - especially when the person is going through traumatic times, emotional upheaval, etc. Other guides have been here many times. Sometimes our guides are relatives who have crossed before us. We have a multitude of guides to help us. Some are with us our whole earth life, others come in for short periods of time - possibly to help with a certain event happening in our life, or to help us reach a goal we've set.

Often, I'll give messages to a person that I don't understand, that seem so totally weird or off, but it's not my job to interpret messages - just to give them as I receive them. The person that I'm talking with will know what it is, but it is not my purpose to know. My job is to be an open and honest channel for Spirit; to just give what I'm given; to not interpret or elaborate.

When I bring through those on the other side, who we knew as friends, relatives, co-workers, etc., I ask that the person

I'm working for remembers how that person was when they were here on the earth plane. I have been shown that when we are in Spirit, our job is to heal from our lives on earth and to grow and learn, and possibly to prepare for our next life. However, when they come to you, they need to come through in a way that you would recognize, so you need to be aware of what they were like on this earth plane. Some people might not agree with me, but if "Uncle Joe" didn't know how to run his finances, you might want to think hard about his advice about your money situation. It doesn't mean he isn't coming from a higher learned perspective and with your best interests in mind. Just go with your gut feelings.

I asked Nicky if that means that you should consider that their information or advice is limited with their personal knowledge.

Again, I'd say to follow your gut feeling about your message. They always want what is best for you. They are always growing and learning. Their job is not to tell us what to do, their job is to prove that life is continuous by coming in and giving you proof that it's them. Sometimes they might give you some advice. I tell people to take the advice, sit with it, and go from there.

The psychic part is where the medium is able to read a person's energy. I find the reading is a combination of your energy and the messages from your guides and loved ones. I consider myself a psychic medium. People want to know that their loved ones are okay, but they also want to know the psychic messages. For example, they want to know where their job is going or what's going on with a relationship. Not to say that your guides and loved ones won't give messages about those parts of your lives; often they will.

One thing that sometimes you hear people ask is, "Oh, how can you believe in that stuff?" Or, "Does it all come true?" We're working with the energies that you have right now, and we all have free will, so something that is in the works now for you could possibly change, especially if there are other people involved. Or something may not happen until everything is lined up the right way. I went to a medium once and she told me that by October that year I was going to meet a special man, and she described him with details, and she added that he had many children. She was right about everything, except the timing was off. That's what people sometimes don't understand is that a medium can tell you where you're heading or that a relationship is right for you or not right for you, but we all have free will. We can change some of these things. And when there are other people involved in the situation, everyone has to be ready too. It's very interesting. Again, it's all about how things fall into place and maybe you weren't ready for it, or other things had to happen before this situation was going to happen. I firmly believe that there are things that we can change and there are situations that must happen to fulfill our reason for coming here, but you might take a longer time to get there, especially if you take a little side road along the way.

Can you explain what you believe happens when someone dies?

What Spirit tells me is that when people cross over, they are immediately welcomed by a spirit family, and then they experience exactly what they had a belief in about the afterlife. For example, if they believed they were going to heaven or hell, then that initial experience will be what they thought it would be. Then, as the person re-acclimates to the spirit world, they remember they are just energy, and they come to the realization that they are back to their true home. When we come to this earth plane, we don't remember our real home and our true spirit. We are here to have the experiences that we previously chose to work on. Now, I've been shown that at this point in crossing over, (I myself don't believe in heaven or hell), there are different levels there. Lower-level energies go to the lower level, and higher energies to higher levels. We all heal and grow so that we can move to higher and higher levels.

There is a place of healing as you review the lifetime that you have just had, and you look at the lessons learned or not learned. Sometimes we don't learn the lessons, and we have to come back and do it again. You slowly heal, and then I believe that if it's meant to be, that you then make decisions about coming back, and who you're going to come back as, and whether you need to work on the same lesson or choose something else.

We grow and heal when we cross over, and we attain higher and higher levels, and at some point, we don't have to come back again. I see a lot of people lately who I would call old souls; people who have been on this earth plane many, many times and have gotten it, and they probably don't have to come back, and they probably will make the choice not to. It is my belief that when spirits don't reincarnate any longer, they become angels or guides for people who are on this earth plane.

Crossing over is a period of being home and healing and learning, just like what we are doing here. We are always learning and growing spiritually. If, for example someone died suddenly in an accident, or if they were murdered, it is a shock to cross over, so there is a lot of help and healing for them there.

Our loved ones who have crossed over can be wherever we are, and they can come to us in a matter of seconds. They are energy, so they can be in one place and they could also be everywhere at the same time. It's hard for us to imagine that reality. There is no time and no space on the other side. I will go one step further and say that a lot of people believe that we are living all our lifetimes at once. Honestly, that just gives me a headache! I have a hard time processing that concept, and I understand that quantum physics says that it's possible. But for me with my human brain, in order to survive here, I think chronologically; that time moves forward; the days, the weeks, the years. Everything is chronological and moving, but in reality, some say, everything is happening at once.

Can you talk about your experience in helping people with past life regressions?

I am a past life regression therapist, and it always fascinates me to see the healing that can happen when people look at their past lives, and how those memories are all attached to us, and how understanding certain patterns can change our lives. I love doing regression work with people, but progression is something I want to learn more about. You might be working on patience or unconditional love, but if you can grasp it and work on and heal all the issues that you need to heal, then you won't have to come back over and over again. You might come back in a different part of a relationship. For example, you could come back as your husband or son or daughter next time, but you would still be working on something in your evolution. It's just fascinating and fun to think about.

I had a lady come to me for a past life regression, and initially I discuss with the client what is happening in this lifetime, and what is it that they want to change. Sometimes people want to stop having the same patterns in relationships over and over again. This lady had infertility issues. The doctor ruled out anything physically wrong with her or her husband, so they weren't sure why they weren't able to get pregnant. I usually set up three sessions for the past life regression. She came to me for the first session and she regressed to lifetimes where she had children, but due to different circumstances wasn't able to take care of them. Either the children died or she died and her children were left alone. There were several situations of lifetimes that she touched on where she couldn't take care of her children. We had a second session and the same themes were coming through, and then we were scheduled for a third session. She called and said, "Hey, I don't need my third session, we are pregnant!" This woman ended up having twins!

There are so many stories, and that's a pretty dramatic one. Another story that comes up is of people finding lifetimes where they couldn't lose weight in this life no matter how hard they tried. They do a past life regression and find out that in other lifetimes, they were so poor they starved. They come to a realization at the end of the session that they over eat because on some unconscious level they fear they will not have enough to eat.

At the end of a session, we work on forgiveness where they forgive themselves and forgive any of the relationships in that lifetime. You have all these people come forward so that you can let go of that stuff. It's pretty intense sometimes.

I told Nicky that I tried years ago to have a past life regression, but I wasn't able to let myself go under hypnosis, and though I feel I might be open more to it now, I have a little anxiety about going and not being able to be regressed again. I have had past life readings, but have never been hypnotized so that I could relive it, and remember it.

Often it takes more than a session, and sometimes I explain to people who are worried that they won't be able to be hypnotized that when you are working with a past life regression therapist like me, it is a very light hypnosis. During the session I ask questions, and I help people to move backwards in this life from one experience back to another, until you're in limbo and then drop into a past life that will help you to understand what it is you want to work on. In that lifetime, you move from one experience to another until the death experience. So, you have to be under light enough that you can speak with me. It's not a deep hypnosis, and if you can meditate at all, or if you can lose yourself in a book so that if someone talks to you, you jump because you're so into the book, or if you can watch television and lose yourself, you can be hypnotized. Or another example is when you drive somewhere and you get lost in thought and suddenly you wonder, how the heck did I get home? That's all similar to the process of being able to be hypnotized.

In 2007, I had a weeklong training on past life regression therapy with a group in West Virginia. After our initial training, we practiced regressing each other and we did this all day long, and there were some amazing breakthroughs, even just in the trainings. Past life regression can just be so powerful, and the amazing thing is that even people who don't believe in reincarnation, who don't believe that they have had many lives, they can still be regressed because it can be memories from this lifetime that are affecting them. When you put it that way to people, they will regress and they will go into their former lives. Even if you think your experience is just a story that you have told yourself, what matters is that you get the healing that you find in recognizing patterns, and you heal those patterns.

The most important things I want to share with everyone are:

1. that life is continuous;

2. that we can communicate with our loved ones on the other side in a variety of ways;

3. that you can do so on your own through meditation, contemplation, asking for connection;

4. that we have Guides who are just waiting for us to ask them for assistance;

5. that we can access our subconscious thoughts and beliefs to help us make this life experience a better one; and

6. that Spirit loves us all - every single one of us. Blessed Be.

I have a full-time day job so I offer mediumship during evenings Monday through Thursday. Weekends are reserved for family and farm. My husband has twelve children and I have two, and we have forty-three grand and great-grandchildren! Life is full!

To contact Nicky for a reading or past life regression, please send an email to: allennicky62@gmail.com
or by phone at 207-344-9259

Chapter 8

Annette Parlin -Medium Clairvoyant, Astral Travel

I have known Annette since 2009 when I met her at a haunted house in Mount Vernon, Maine, while collecting ghost stories for my first book, <u>Hauntings from Wayne and Beyond</u>. Annette was a friend of the homeowner and she shared stories about the ghosts and spirits she sensed there. Annette agreed to visit other haunted houses with me while I did research for the book, and she was able to verify the homeowners' stories, help them understand their hauntings, and sometimes assisted the ghosts with crossing over. Annette is a remarkable medium clairvoyant who gives private and group psychic readings, as well as house readings. I have received very specific messages from loved ones in my readings with Annette over the years and I highly recommend her. She is a truly unique, interesting, and gifted old soul.

It was thrilling and surreal to have Annette go along with me to visit the amazing old haunted houses to collect stories for all three of my ghost books: <u>Hauntings from Wayne and Beyond,</u> <u>Hauntings from Wayne and Beyond 2</u>, and <u>Hauntings from</u>

Eastport and Beyond. I learned a lot from Annette about the spirit world and over the years we have become close friends.

A natural storyteller, I have always enjoyed hearing about Annette's incredible personal experiences with spirits, ghosts, and other realms, and I was especially fascinated with her personal stories about astral travelling. Annette is a very magical person! The following is from a recorded interview:

I am a medium clairvoyant and have been connected to the spirit world ever since I was a little girl. I saw my first two spirits when I was just ten years old; a man and a woman sitting next to one another, and I could hear them talking, and it was about me! That experience opened up my mind to connect more with spirits as I grew up.

My gifts first came in dreams and sometimes a "knowing" that would later come to fruition. My mother was psychic, and some of my siblings were too, and later I realized both sides of my family were very gifted. It was and is generational. It was fun sharing these unusual experiences with family and friends and in doing so, it became natural. As the years went by, my gifts became stronger, and I began to experience things that sometimes left me frightened and confused. I didn't understand some of what I was seeing, hearing and experiencing. I became very close to a woman who was extremely intuitive and she helped me understand my gifts. She became my mentor, and I am forever grateful to her.

I was able to go into the future and watch a scene, and then come back and see it played out. I began to see people I didn't know, and then I was able to hear them speak and they would answer me. Eventually I was able to hold conversations with ghosts and loved ones that had passed.

I learned to embrace my gifts, seeking more knowledge so I could have a better understanding of the connection to the Divine, and seek answers as time went on, working only in light and love.

I realized that I could share my experiences and help others understand the spirit world. From there I branched out to doing psychic readings, and since I could see ghosts and spirits too, I branched out even more by doing ghost investigations. It has been a magical and delightful journey!

I had heard of astral traveling and always wondered what it was all about and how it worked. I didn't know much about it until I started going places myself. I had been on a spiritual journey the last few years to try to connect more with the universe, to grow more with the oneness of it all. The more I experienced, the more vastness I was discovering, experiencing different realms and reality. It is all endless! There is no way one will ever understand it all. We are only able to experience just a small sliver of it. I am in awe of it all. My travels have been magical, and I am thankful to have these incredible experiences, as they are now a part of my spiritual journey in this life.

One of my first experiences happened when my husband Ronnie and I were enjoying a local outdoor concert at a gazebo in Farmington. There were Native American drummers performing and someone was playing the flute. Ronnie and I were just there to experience the nice music, but the drumming moved me, as I always felt a connection with Native American people. I felt inspired to close my eyes and as I focused on the music and the drumming, the next thing I knew, I could see myself as a Native American woman standing in this vast field of tall grass. The wind was whipping so hard that my braided pigtails were slapping and stinging my face, and I felt my deerskin skirt flapping hard against my legs. I saw nothing but fields as far as I could see. I could smell something wonderful, and I realized I was standing in a field of sweet grass.

I opened up my eyes and turned to Ronnie and said, "Oh my God, that's really cool. I just went somewhere! I think I just astral traveled!"

Another time Ronnie and I were in the car and driving down the highway and I had a citrine crystal with me, and I was just learning about its energies. My husband said to me, "Why don't you take your citrine out and see if you can astral travel with it?"

I took it out of my bag and held it in my hands and closed my eyes. Suddenly, I saw myself in front of our car on the highway and my face was just inches from the road, and somehow, I was flying as fast as the car, hovering just above the road! I did not have wings, but I was flying! I thought to myself, *if I can fly, why am I stuck down here?* Then, just as I had that thought, I was flying. Suddenly I had wings, and I was up very high in the sky! I was having so much fun with the freedom! Then flying to my left, I saw a Golden eagle, which has always been important to me spiritually. He flew just a few feet in front of me, and he bellied up and put his talons out towards me, and so I bellied up too and took my bare feet to his talons and we were playing footsies! I sensed he was a male eagle and I thought he was a very high eagle or symbolic of a higher source. It was extremely thrilling, and then the eagle let go and he flew back the same way he came.

All of a sudden, the scene switched and I'm a little girl and I am with my father. Now, I personally believe we have a true family on the other side who can be different from who our family are here. In this vision I am with my true father. I see the action of an arm going up and down, and up and down, and it was my father shoeing a horse. When the vision pans out more, I'm a little girl about five years old, and I am wearing little shoes with little ankle stockings and a little dress. It is summer, and I get the impression that my father is talking to two men and he's bartering with them. Then, it's time to leave, and I am aware that I love my father very much. I raise my hands for him to pick me up, but he ignores that and grabs my hand gently. I think, *I'm a big girl. I don't need to be picked up.* Then we walked together hand-in-hand to a buckboard, and that's very symbolic and has come up many times in readings and dreams for me. A buckboard is a horse pulled open wagon sometimes with no railings. This buckboard had no railings on it, so my father lifted me up and sat me down on the bench. He got in and I sat next to him, and he pulled up the reins and told the horse to go. I hugged my father and felt so much love for him. He took out a pipe and started smoking it. I could smell the beautiful scent of the tobacco and we started heading off, and then the vision ended. I came out of the experience with just the feeling of how much I loved my father. I said to Ronnie,

"You will never believe where I went." I told him the whole story, and he said,

"Your father lit a pipe, and it was pipe tobacco?" I said,

"Yes." Ronnie said,

"Just about when you were ending your meditation, I could smell pipe tobacco. I thought maybe it was the car in front of us." I can't explain it, but I love the mystery of it all.

I truly feel that, for example, when I was the Native American woman, I was getting a glimpse of a past life, but I know I went somewhere to a different plane or realm. Another part of that past life experience was that I was sitting with other women in the shadows on green grass, and it was so realistic that I could feel details like the dew of the grass. Off to the right, the Native American men were all dancing around a fire. We were watching them, and they were doing a dance ceremony because they were going on a big hunt the next day to hunt bison. We women were not allowed to join in because it wasn't for women. I could hear the crackling of the fire and also the drumming in the music.

The astral traveling comes easy for me now, and I have come to feel that it is unlimited, and anything is possible. Whatever reality we create, becomes real.

I wanted to experience a Reiki session, as I had never had one before in my life, and I went to my gifted friend Pam because I knew I needed healing for a knee issue. She worked on my knee, hoping to heal it so I wouldn't need to have surgery, but I ended up having a total knee replacement afterward anyway. Pam wanted to explore why I was having the knee issue, and she asked me if I had brought this issue in from a previous life. I didn't believe it was a past life issue because I knew something about my past lives. She asked me if I could ask my guides to help me find the answer, so I asked my guides for assistance. Right then I had a vision of myself sitting at a very ancient wooden table. I look around and there in front of me was the biggest, oldest looking book I've ever seen, and it was laying open on the table. I had an understanding that this was a book of all the lives I've ever lived. It was left open for me to look up in my recent past to see if I had knee issues. At this point, I looked up to my left, and in through a round door comes in a huge wizard who looks exactly like Gandalf from the Lord of the Rings! He had to bend over to come in the doorway because he was much taller than the door. He came in and it was my understanding that he was going to sit in my place and guard this open book of all of my lives since the beginning. I understood it was to protect my privacy from other energies that might want to look in. So, he sat down where I was sitting and I walked out through the door and left.

The next thing I knew, I was flying up in the sky somewhere. I'm not sure where, but I was going very, very high, and suddenly I was at the top of a mountain, and I looked all around. All the mountains were identical and had very sharp, dark peaks. It made me think of an Asian photograph. They were all black around me and I knew I was as high as I could get on this earth. There to my right was a cave, and sitting outside the cave was a man, and he looked like a shaman or some kind of high priestess. He was wearing a hood and he sat with his legs crossed. I don't remember speaking with words, but I knew he was very, very high and that it was an honor to be where I was. He gave me the understanding that my knee issue was not a past life issue. Then, the vision ended abruptly. I looked at Pam who was still working on my knee and I said, "No, it's not a continuation of a knee issue from a previous life." I told her where I had gone and she said,

"You've got to be kidding. You went to look at your own Akashic records!"

I didn't know what that was and I had to look it up. I learned that the Akashic records experience differs from person to person, but as humans we think of it as a library of books and it exists on the ethereal plane. It is a record of all that has happened in each person's lifetimes and has been recorded into a book. I thought it was interesting that mine needed to be guarded, but I understand from it that each life is very sacred and needs protection.

During a different healing session with Pam, I also learned about the concept of our higher self. I didn't know what that was previously. I wasn't conscious of it, but during that particular session, when I was relaxing and enjoying it, I was aware I felt very tired. I was thankful to be receiving Pam's beautiful energy, and the next thing I know, I heard my higher self say, "Pam, let me give you some of my energy." I was totally shocked. I thought, *What am I talking about? I'm the one who needs healing!* And I hear my higher self say back,

"You have an abundance of energy!" Then I hear my higher self say to Pam, "Let me show you where I live."

Next thing I know, I am flying and I go to a place that looks again like the Shire from the Hobbit. Everything was green and vibrant and surreal. The colors were stunning. I heard my higher self say to Pam, "This is where I live!" Then I said to myself, questioning,

"I live here?" My higher self answered back by repeating the scene again. I went to the Hobbit place again and my higher self repeated,

"Pam this is where I live." I thought, maybe this is where I live when I go in between my lives on earth.

About fifteen years ago I was asked to join a dear friend of mine who was going to have a past life regression session, and she asked me to go along for support. I was so overjoyed to have the opportunity to sit in on her session because I had never experienced that before. During the session, my friend was having trouble regressing back. The therapist suggested she relax and use visualizations, and to specifically imagine herself in a gazebo, to hopefully open up the astral plane in the fifth dimension and see what happens from there. That was all new to me and I thought, *oh, interesting, you can put yourself somewhere and use that for a focal point, and then you can go wherever you want to go!* That was my very first experience with learning about astral travelling, and it opened up a big door for me.

My sisters, Therese and Diane, my husband Ronnie, and my friend Paula are also intuitive and psychic, and we talked about astral travelling and decided that if it is possible to meditate and envision oneself in a special place like a gazebo and astral travel from there, then perhaps we could do that on our own without the hypnotherapist. We talked about trying to meditate and to see what we could experience, and sharing it with each other.

In a meditation I visualized my gazebo made out of logs and wood, with a thatched roof and a birdhouse on top. This gazebo was very deep in the woods and I designed it that way because I wanted the gazebo to be a sacred place that was just mine. There I imagined I could travel into the past, or go to the future; whatever I desired.

My husband, my sisters, and friend also created their own gazebos, but we did not share with each other the details or description of our special sacred places. We wanted to test if the experience was real, by travelling and visiting each other's gazebos, and reporting back. My husband designed a log cabin, my sister Diane made hers in a seashell on the seashore, Theresa made hers in a swamp, and Paula had a unique gazebo as well.

So, we texted one night and we invited each other to visit our gazebos or special places. We were amazed at what happened. Paula went to my husband's place, without knowing it was a log cabin, and she not only accurately described how he designed his cabin, she said that she saw other details such as a field with yellow flowers everywhere, and saw there was water in the front, so that you had to walk over rocks to get to it. She added that when she looked at the left side of the cabin, she couldn't see anything. When she shared that with my husband, he said, "Well, of course not, I haven't created it yet!"

We were amazed and excited because the experience taught us that the special places we each created in our meditations somehow became real places! It was unbelievable, and at first, we kept this incredible experience among our special little group.

None of us knew anyone who had such experiences and we had never read about anything like this before or heard other psychics mention this. I would love to talk with anyone who has. We found it very interesting, and we decided to have past life regressions done by a local hypnotist. We told her what we were experiencing, and also it came up during our past life regressions with her, because I could get validation from going to the other side and I would describe these meetings. We explained about how we tested each other by going to each other's places, and we asked her if that was normal; and was it real? The hypnotist said that it was not something she ever heard of before and that we were teaching her about a whole other aspect of reality.

I have so many stories to share but I want to end by saying that I love the mystical experiences of astral traveling, and it has been an astonishing learning experience for me. I know that my experiences are just a little piece of the puzzle and there is so much more to learn. There are so many aspects of reality and time, past, present and future, and the many realms of existence. I am only beginning to learn, and I am very thankful for it all.

To contact Annette for a private psychic reading, or ghost investigation, email her at psychicannette@hotmail.com or call 207-779-6114

Chapter 9

Jennifer Laflin - Spiritual Medium
and Psychic Intuitive

Jennifer Laflin is an extraordinary and remarkable spiritual medium and psychic intuitive. She brings forth details and deep insights in her readings, has an understanding of the complexities of the human psyche, and with her very engaging personality, is extremely entertaining during a gallery reading. If you ever get the chance to join in on one of her gallery reading sessions, she has the ability to raise the vibration of the room with her quick wit and humor, helpful when delivering messages that can sometimes be emotional. She also gives good advice for anyone having a spiritual reading for the first time.

It is interesting to note that many of Jennifer's clients are referred to her by their therapist. She explained that many clients are unable to move forward in their therapy due to the pain of bringing up raw feelings about trauma or abuse.

When I see a client who has been referred to me by their therapist, they are initially nervous, not knowing what to expect from a spiritual medium. They size me up at first, and I say to them, "Now that you're done sizing me up, are you comfortable?" They usually start laughing and then say,

"You picked up on that?" It's a nice icebreaker and within five minutes or so we're dealing with some pretty intense stuff. They frequently say, "You hit on everything that I had questions about and needed to know."

When I first meet with a referred client, I am able to get their attention as they are initially stunned by the incredible insights that come through. The minute the client is engaged in the reading, I can quickly address their feelings and emotions because, as an empath, I am able to connect with them and feel their pain whether it be physical or verbal abuse, despair, or trauma. The therapist is not always privy to that information, but for me, the minute the client opens up, we are able to start a very real and honest conversation.

At this point, the client can be emotional because they feel relieved that they don't have to talk about the tender issue, and as a spiritual medium and empath, I am able to provide validation for the pain they have been through. I always recommend clients record the session so that they can go back and continue the discussion with their therapist, and that will hopefully help them move further along in their therapy sessions.

I try to tell people that you really don't have to fix everything, you just have to alter it. That's what life is about. It's about recognizing your role in your life.

Pleasantly surprised to learn that there are therapists who are open to the healing of mediumship, I asked Jennifer how therapists find out about her.

The therapists who refer their clients to me usually have had readings with me before. A lot of my advertisement is by word of mouth. I've had a wide clientele, and I've read people from all walks of life. I am grateful to be able to read people distantly everywhere in the United States and beyond. Everyone was originally a client, or a referral from a client.

Whenever I finish a reading, I tell the person that everything becomes erased for me. I don't remember any of it, even if I've read you five times, I won't remember any details the next time I talk to you. It is a good thing because they (clients)

don't want me to have a preconceived notion of where they were at during a prior reading. I think it is because the spirits who come through want me to have a clean slate with the person every single time. So, I go in there with that knowledge, and I don't write anything down about my clients. I say to them when I begin a session that if there's a particular question or anything that you want to know, ask me at any time during the reading. If there's anyone in particular you want to hear from, just give me the person's first name; I don't need a last name. I also tell them to please interrupt me if they have questions, even if I am in the middle of a sentence; it doesn't break my train of thought.

Sometimes there is so much growth from when I first meet a client, from when they were filled with sadness and grief and their sense of loss was great. For the spirit coming through, it is a balancing act to make sure their loved ones are okay. The loved one in spirit wants to help the client work through the grieving, and when the client grieves, the spirit keeps coming back to them to reassure them that they are okay where they are. In all reality, the spirit needs to grow on the other side but is unable to, if drawn into the person's deep sorrow.

I have noticed that readings have changed over the years. People come to me more often now to work on personal issues. It used to be more about wanting to connect with a loved one in spirit. Now people want to know if they are on the right track in their lives. It's more about their self-improvement and wanting a meaningful change because they're tired of the old way of doing things.

Some people tell me, "I want a new way of looking at life. I will die if I continue the way I am going." Many people are depressed and they are looking for someone to say it is okay, instead of judging them for how they feel. I find that with many people I talk to these days, they are tired of the nonhuman touch. People are tired of the isolation. It's like my daughter-in-law said recently, that the kids today are constantly on their iPhones and iPads and they are losing touch of what it means to go outside and play a game with the neighborhood kids. Children and teenagers are growing up more isolated and not learning to negotiate simple face to face communication skills. They are not learning interpersonal skills like being able to pick up on body language and vibes we get from each other in relationships.

I find that there are a lot of people who are introverted and sensitive, and also empaths. I am a psychic medium and a strong empath, and I notice that many empaths pick up on other people's emotions such as anger, and do not realize it doesn't belong to them. It's not their anger they feel, it is another person around them who is angry. Empathic people need to recognize that sometimes it's not their energy and emotions they are feeling, that it is another person's energy they are sensing.

I have taught people who are very empathic to ask themselves, is it yours or is it somebody else's energy you are feeling? When you stand next to somebody and begin getting a feeling, move your body away from them a little or just turn your body slightly, and then see if you can tell if it's your energy or someone else's that you are sensing.

I asked Jennifer how she gets her information from Spirit during the reading, something I'm always curious about when talking to mediums.

It's hard to explain, because each energy form that comes through has a different way of communicating. I hear, see, and feel things, and I have a sense of knowing. It's a definite knowing, almost as if I am that person and I know it to be true. Each individual, spirit, or energy that comes through in a reading has a unique form of communication. A client may have different energies that come through, and they communicate in different ways for me. I am always adapting to the way in which I get information. I have to figure out how to line up with and interpret the conversation with the person or spirit that is with me.

For instance, sometimes a spirit will come in with other family members who are similar in their behaviors, such as being loving and caring. I might sense they are one person, until the client says, "Oh that sounds like my aunt."

Then I might separate the spirits by "putting" them in separate places in my office, so that I can become clearer about who they were as an individual and what their journey is or was. There's just this strong sense of knowing that the information I get is right when I'm in a conversation with them. I need to completely remove who I am, my ego, as well as my sense of past, present, and future. It is important that I try to exist where the energy from the other side is at.

I have given readings to people and they have laughed, cried, and they were wholeheartedly engaged in the reading, and then at the end they say something like, "Can you tell me what my mother's nickname for me was?"

It is as if they are saying to the spirits, "I want to hear from you," but then they shut the door. They do not trust that the message is real. I understand skepticism, but I just think the person is missing out on an opportunity. To have an optimal experience in a reading, the client must trust and work with their guides and the medium, for best results.

The information that your spirit guides give you is what they feel is the best for you from their perspective. You as a human may not see that because you don't have the same perspective, and if it's not the direct response to your question, you might set it aside. However, years down the road you might think back and realize that what your guides were telling you was correct. Many times, people don't understand the message that they're getting from their guides. They may ask the question and when an answer is given, the person doubts it. When you're asking your spirit guides a question, they are giving you the exact response to what you require at that time. My advice is to have faith in what they are saying, and know that their answer may come in many forms.

When I talk to my spirit guides, or any energies that I connect to, it sometimes takes me a couple of days to mull it over. Even I question the message that comes to me from my spirit guides from time to time. However, it is important to know that when your guides come to you, it is for you to become the highest form of yourself. You asked them before you were born to be there for you and to help with your growth. Because of this, they will have a world of patience with you.

On a personal level, it is not always easy living with these gifts. As a medium it can be tough having friends and "knowing" things, and making the separation between pulling apart the medium and who I am. For myself, I never shut down. I am both me the human and the spiritual medium and that's all I ever want to be. I have had to ask friends ahead of time that if a message were to come through, whether or not they want me to tell them. I feel if a message comes up and I didn't tell the friend that I would feel guilty if they didn't get the message that was intended for them. Sometimes friends say they don't want to take advantage of what I do, but I tell them they are not taking advantage if I give it freely. I have friends who are gifted mediums who will give a message to me in the middle of a conversation, and I am grateful for any information that is required for me to know at that time. But as a medium, I sometimes question whether I should share information I get or not, so I always ask for permission first.

Can you explain about how you became aware of your psychic gifts?

I knew I was different around the age of three or four, and I remember feeling alone and like I didn't belong. My father was a very strong Catholic and we dutifully went to church every Sunday, so I have that religious background. When I was eleven years old, my grandfather died and that's when I saw my first three ghosts. They all came to me at the same time, and it terrified me. I couldn't talk about that experience because I was brought up during the times when it was best for children to be seen, but not heard. I kept things to myself. As time went on, I grew up, got married and had a family. I didn't develop my psychic skills until later, though I had taken a few classes here and there. I also tried my hand at doing tarot card readings, but I was told I was reading the cards as a medium, and that I shouldn't do that. It was later after I was divorced that Iconnected with a mentor and I told her that I was ready to do mediumship, and the rest is history. I went to psychic fairs and started building a clientele, and now I do mediumship full time and I work out of an office.

My life wasn't always easy. Did all the ups and downs I went through make me who I am now? Absolutely. It cracked me open to what I needed to work on. I truly love what I do, and I have been doing it full-time since 2015. I like to help people work on certain aspects of themselves, whether spiritually or mentally.

I offer personal, group, and pet readings, and I teach mediumship on different levels, and I offer various workshops as well. I offer a group which meets once a month and is meant to provide free conversation about any spiritual topic, and it has been very popular. I have a class on mentorship and I enjoy working with people on finding out who they are as a person, and how to embrace it. I don't teach by the book; I teach by the person and what they need. I also do psychometry and dream interpretation. I am thankful for my gifts and my life as a medium.

During the interview Jennifer gave me some important insights about my life, particularly on my habit of dropping everything when someone needs my help, to the point that I give away too much of my energy and become worn down by it. I was impressed with the accurate details that Jennifer came up with about my life. My reading was excellent, and Jennifer told me that part of my healing at this point in my life was to learn that I am on my own journey, and that my children, who are young adults are each on their own journeys. She said that I will soon find peace in that knowledge. I believe she said this because when we watch our loved ones going through hard stuff, as I have with my children, sometimes, no matter how much we pray and ask for help for them, they need to go through the hard lessons for their own development and growth. That information and message helped me more than I can say.

To contact Jennifer for a reading, group or class, please go to her website: www.jenniferlaflin.com.

Chapter 10

Brenda Colfer - Reiki Soundings-Holistic Massage

The moment I walked into Brenda's studio I immediately felt at ease with her easygoing vibe. We talked about her gifts and sound healing, as she demonstrated her gongs, rattles, crystal bowls, didgeridoos and more. It was both fascinating and healing just to meld with Brenda's light energy and resonate with the beautiful sounds in the sacred space of her studio. I quickly understood how beautiful and powerful sound healing can be.

I see all my clients in one room now. My new lift table allows me to be able to offer Holistic Massage for Women, Reiki with Sound, and Craniosacral and Lymphatic Drainage in the same room. I don't offer straight massage. My Holistic Massage continues to morph, allowing for more space for energy work, lymphatic work, craniosacral, crystals and sound. After my training in massage therapy, I found that as I started with my massage sessions, I was drawn to offer energy work first. Tuning forks, or my Himalayan Bowls, placed on the body allow for a quick shift and releases the energy that we are working on.

Craniosacral, Lymphatic Drainage, Reiki, Essential Oils, Crystals, etc. may all be part of the massage.

When I work with someone who has come in for a Reiki Sound Session, I will begin with an intake. This can take anywhere from a half hour to an hour, because we are figuring out where we are going to go during the session and what they would like to work on.

Before the client arrives, I also pull a couple of Divination cards and tap into any intuitive insights. Part of my process is seeing my client in my mind's eye, and I will put them on a dirt road to see how they are moving forward in life. Sometimes I see that they are stuck in mud, or facing backwards focusing on the past, or they may be in the middle of a sacred pause when it isn't time to move forward. I find many of my clients come because they are looking for help in an area of their life where they are feeling stuck. I also often put people in what I call the room. In the room I ask to be shown what it is that they need to have worked on today.

I share this information with my client during their intake. It is a formula that I have worked with for many years. Once we are ready for table time, I wash my hands to prepare for the session. I start to get insights often during this process. When I approach my client, who is now resting on a massage table, I listen to their field. Our energy fields merge before we touch. My thought is what does this person need from me today... and then I listen to their field. This will tell me where to begin and how to start. Sometimes I begin with just being supportive and I sit with them and hold/touch them throughout, and there are times when I don't bring sound into it. I have had sessions where I haven't touched the client at all. You just never know how it is going to play out until you're in it. There are times when I start with the sounds of my crystal singing bowls, or my rattle or another instrument that is calling to me.

Looking around the room, I notice a very large brass gong and I admired how beautiful it was.

I use my gongs on sound night and in private sessions. I have this large one set up and tilted towards the massage table so that it will wash over the client as I play it. It is interesting because it is still teaching me. Every tool teaches you the same way a stone teaches you. You learn to ask how it wants to be used in a session. As I have worked with the gongs, I have come to realize that part of their gift is to help release fear. I don't want to limit its ability, and I don't want to label it, but I do notice patterns, and fear is part of the component that the gong works on. Sometimes when I'm working, I see the clients face on the gong and will tap the gong where the face shows up. It is about listening with your feet and your hands, and where my feet want to take me in the room. If I am holding a drum, I think, *where am I guided to go?* I listen to my hands. I feel as if my hands know so much more than I do. There is me, and then there's my hands. I just think there is so much more knowledge and wisdom there, and it's just about dropping in and listening to it.

I ask if fear and anxiety are the most common issues people have these days.

Yes, anxiety is very common especially with remnants of Covid. People come for a variety of reasons, and sometimes they may not even be aware of why they want to come. Sometimes it is for a healing because there is something specific going on physically, emotionally, mentally, or spiritually. At times they are looking for a better connection to themselves or to the Divine. Reiki can bring people into such deep stillness where they can make that beautiful connection. Often, they come because they feel stuck in some area of their life. It seems to me that my calling is to help people to move forward in life.

I asked Brenda to describe herself and her gifts.

I am trained in Reiki. I have a great respect for the realm of Reiki. I don't typically use the title Reiki Master; it just doesn't fit with me. I just have too much respect for the energy. I like the title Reiki Teacher. There are other modalities that I can claim Master level, but not with Reiki. There is just something very sacred about Reiki for me. I have had many trainings over the years. Hypnotherapy, Integrated Energy Therapy, Biodynamic Craniosacral, Quantum-Touch, and Reflexology. These modalities are woven into my current work, but I don't offer as a stand-alone session. Lymphatic Drainage, Craniosacral, and Vibrational Sound

Therapy also may be woven into my sessions, but can also be a stand-alone session. When I turned sixty, I began my training in massage therapy.

I also offer LifeBreath, which is phenomenal. It is a beautiful modality of deep breathing. The class usually takes two hours. During the class I will talk about what to do and how to do it, what you might experience, and set our intentions. We typically will set intentions for your breath experience, or what kind of miracle do you want to create, or what do you want to bring into your life. I ask for the students to put their intention in a positive frame. For example, if a person was experiencing anger, instead of saying "I want to breathe to release anger," I ask the person, "If you were to release the anger what would that look like; what would that be?" They might say peace, and that would be their intention. I breath for peace.

LifeBreath is often done in group format, but it can also be done on an individual basis. Breath work is like a meditation. It is hard to describe. The deep breathing brings you into an altered state of reality. You may see things, hear things, know things, or feel things that you aren't aware of on a conscious level. People often have big experiences with LifeBreath. Breath is Spirit. One of the best things about breath work is that it brings forth clarity. On so many different levels, the breath offers to detox with the exhale and to fully oxygenate the cells of our bodies on the inhale; it assists us to move through and to release our stuck emotions; mentally it brings forth great clarity and creates the opportunity to go on an amazing spiritual journey to yourself, or Source, or somewhere in between.

I play the music loudly, so that it sort of hides what's going on, and it also gives the person who is there permission to have their experience. For me, when I am a breather, I laugh, and I laugh so hard that there are tears rolling down my face, and I am having the best time of my life! Some people will laugh, some people will cry. I also find that sometimes people feel more present with themselves, more present than they may ever have been in their whole life, or they may be having a conversation with the Divine. It's fun, and for years I've been calling it Soundings LifeBreath. I bring a variety of sound to play. I may weave in a drum or tuning forks, or I may play a bowl or gong.

SpiritDance developed out of this because during breath work sometimes you just want to get up and move. For about ten years or so, I held a Soundings LifeBreath the last Friday night of the month at a local studio. At the end of one class, I suddenly felt an awareness coming over me that was our last class. I announced to everyone that this may be our last class. Some of the students had been with me since my training. The next awareness that dropped in was that I realized it was just that we were morphing into SpiritDance. So, it became a dance breath class. So, the very next class we started the class out like a LifeBreath class, but stood and danced while we did the breath work. Dancing is a great way to move stuck energy!

I also offer ChakraTribe classes. This night is a moving meditation class where we journey through the chakra's elements. earth, water, fire, air, ether, sound, and light.

I offer Crystal Singing Bowl Meditations often at Maine General and at different studios in the surrounding area.

I also offer Sound Healing or Soundscape nights which incorporate my crystal bowls, Himalayan Bowls, didgeridoo, gongs, and other instruments.

I had to ask Brenda what a didgeridoo was.

When I put people on the road to see what's happening with them, if I get the impression that they are not grounded, or if their feet are not on the ground and they are floating, I will play my didgeridoo to ground them. As I play the didgeridoo I am connecting to the ground and seeing the relationship the client's feet have with the ground. Often when someone is ungrounded, the earth below their feet may energetically appear hard. As I play the didge, I can see the ground softening and their energetic connection to the earth becoming stronger. I play until I feel that it is complete. The didgeridoo is an Aboriginal instrument that is hollowed out from a tree.

I have a Grandmother Grounding Bowl that clients get to step into. I typically use this after each Reiki session to ground the client to make sure they are okay to drive after the session. Sometimes the bowl is used before the session to ground. Everyone is different and responds differently to the bowl. Most ground, but some are drawn upwards.

I notice the Native American flute playing in the background music while we talked, and I mentioned to Brenda that I truly love it and resonate with it.

I always play Native American flute music during my intakes. I do drum during my sessions. For me drumming helps to move and shift energy. I used to use my drums during my journey classes years ago. I have several drums, and again I will listen to see what drum wants to be used, listen to where my feet want to be when I play it, and listen to my hands to see what beat wants to be played. Sometimes it is an honoring beat, it may be a heartbeat, or it may be a faster journey beat. The client can feel the vibrations of the drum as it is played above them.

Brenda demonstrated drumming as she stood behind me. It was very moving, and I understood how powerful drumming can be.

I offer Vibrational Sound Therapy, which means the sound is placed physically on the body. It is extremely relaxing to have the metal bowls (Himalayan) played on the body.

Brenda demonstrated for me the feeling and the sound of more of her instruments. She showed me an ocean drum, a Shruti box and a tuning fork. She demonstrated her rain stick which she plays at the end of the session, and she explained it purifies and is like a wash over the person. I loved all of the sound healing examples.

I know Reiki can stand on its own and it doesn't need all of this. I like variety, so the sound helps to engage my intuition and keeps me excited about offering sessions. Even though I know the Reiki doesn't need it, I find it helps to move things along quicker allowing me to do more. There is a sweetness added with the sound healing.

Brenda also played some chimes that she uses near the end of a session, which felt very light and beautiful. We talked about the lovely sounds of nature, like the songs of the birds and the frogs in the spring, which are also healing, she said.

Natural sounds are beautiful, and nature is the biggest healer. I always think that a lumberjack would never need to be here for a session because they are out in nature all the time. They are filled and connected to nature daily.

If you had told me thirty years ago that I would be doing intuitive Reiki and Sound Healing, I wouldn't have believed it. I woke up one morning knowing something I didn't want to know, and six months later we found out that my father had cancer. Besides my intuitive feelings of knowing things, like, get out of the party now because the cops are coming! (Laughter.) That kind of knowing I have always had, and it came in handy. But that morning, I woke up and knew things were never going to be the same. That was the first time I ever had a real sense of knowing. After I found out my father had cancer, I started taking meditation classes in Augusta. On the very first night a woman did a meditation on chakras, and I remember sitting in the class and breathing in the color, as if I was gasping, I was so depleted. I started going to the classes and it helped me to be strong enough so I could be there for my father.

One night they had a guest teacher who spoke of Polarity Healing. I went home and was guided to reach out to have a session with her. Her work also helped me to be there for my dad. I will also remember that first session with her. She had singing bowls, tuning forks, and crystals. It was heaven! She became my teacher. I took Usui Tibetan Reiki with her as well as Karuna Reiki. I didn't set out to do this line of work. I never knew what I wanted to be when I grew up. It wasn't until my first Reiki class, when I was thirty-eight years old, that I finally knew. I just stood there and cried in class. I feel that my father's ordeal was a catalyst for me to find my path.

Have you ever seen spirits or ghosts?

I have seen spirits so real that I didn't know they were spirits at first. I was sitting in my office at work one day and a car came up. A woman got out and walked up to the door. She was wearing jeans, a white shirt and held a purse, and I thought, *oh my gosh, she's going to knock on the door and interrupt the yoga class!* I quickly got up to answer the door to greet her. When I opened the door, she wasn't there. I walked around the building looking for her and her white car, but there wasn't any sign of her or her car. It was so real.

Another time I had a client who left something at my office. I was presenting that night and told her she could meet me there if she wanted to get it sooner. That night my friend and I had created a labyrinth for people to walk through. I was busy when my client showed up. I noticed that she had come in with two children, a boy and a girl with winter coats on. The labyrinth was made of string, and her children were looking at it. I remember thinking, *please be careful, don't let your children step on the strings*. When I was done doing what I was doing, I walked over to my client to give her what she had left behind. I asked her where her children had gone because they were no longer with her. She said, "What kids? I don't have any children with me."

I asked the people at the registration table, and no one had seen any kids there that night. Again, it was so real, it was just like I could reach out and touch them. There was another time when I saw a half a person. I was walking down the stairs and could see someone standing near the railing... I turned to look, and I could see brown penny loafers and brown pants but no upper body with it!

I also use Essential Oils during my sessions. I can offer AromaTouch and Symphony of the Cells. AromaTouch has the same protocol every time, and Symphony of the Cells has many different protocols that work with different systems of the body. Depending on the protocol, the client may or may not have to smell the oils. My massages are changing, and I am not offering the whole protocol for SOC's now. I intuit four oils from the protocols that want to come forward now.

Using essential oils can be an anointing. It is a slow process because we are having a conversation with the central nervous system. When I touch the body, I am having this conversation within where I am saying something like... *the emergency is over, everything is okay now*. I then allow the CNS to dictate how quickly the oil is introduced to the body. My hand will move slowly if needed. There are times when you need to stop moving and linger, and then begin again. It is fun to offer, and it smells wonderful too. The protocol for inflammation and the one for building up the immune system seems to be the most popular ones offered. Sometimes hot packs are offered with the oils, and this takes the process to a whole new level. It's wonderful.

I ask Brenda if healing goes through her when she does a healing for someone.

Yes, you do receive as you give healing. I am a channel for Reiki to flow, so it flows into and through my body. I have to be careful with my balance. Time for me, for my family, for work. I need time in nature, and I need my space. I only see one or two clients a day, and I spread them out. I also need to express this part of me through sessions and classes. It is important to take care of yourself first when doing this kind of work. I want to be able to come into my sessions with curiosity, excitement, and joy. If I did too many sessions in a row, I would quickly become disenchanted.

I put it out there that I only want to attract people who are ready to receive what I have to offer. I speak with the client's higher self and ask to be shown what is ready to be released. If something shows up in the session to work with, I know it is ready to be dealt with. The clients' higher selves are always in charge of the session. Of course, if the client has mentioned something during the intake that they would like to address, I will make sure I honor that area.

After the visit and interview, I later returned for a healing session, which is hard to find the words to describe. I loved, loved, loved every minute of it and visualized Brenda like a Native American medicine woman working magic over and through me with her mixture of Reiki and Shamanism and musical instruments. I highly recommend Brenda to anyone open to this experience.

For more information, please go to Brenda's website at www.reikisoundings.com.

Chapter 11

Regina Strongheart -Medical Intuitive
Spiritual Teacher and Healer

Regina uses Shamanic journeying and past life readings in her healing work. She offers workshops on many cultural and spiritual topics, as well as healing and support groups at her center, Forest Circles, in Topsham, Maine. I found Regina's experiences to be fascinating and her wisdom inspiring. As a lover of the outdoors and the forest myself, I was intrigued by Regina's connection to the earth and the magical healing that it provides. The following stories come from our interview and illustrate Regina's extraordinary gifts and abilities.

I grew up in New Hampshire, went to college, and ultimately became a chemistry and biology teacher for thirty years. I met my husband during the college years and we had three children. After ten years together we divorced, and I became involved with a group of women doing counseling together. We were learning about emotional healing through meditation. This was around 1987, and I continued to be friends with these women.

Later I became more serious about meditation and I delved into New Age spirituality, and read dozens of books on the subject. That's when things started to happen to me; energetic things started happening to my body, spontaneously. I felt energy surges and had experiences where I traveled out of my body. Continuously, my goal was to heal myself, heal myself, heal myself.

I have always been a nature person and I had become a biology and chemistry teacher, so the earth was always very special to me. That continued, and in the early '90s, I began to work with another meditation group which made me even more sensitive to energy. I didn't see myself as a healer then, but around that time I purchased a new home and one room in that house evolved into a healing room. Soon I had an overwhelming impulse to put my hands on people and maybe help them to heal. It turned out that I had a huge amount of energy coming through me that I could pass on to others. I considered taking classes because my friends were calling me a healer. I thought, *okay, I am a healer*. However, I never actually took any classes because Spirit/The Universe was always preventing me from making that call. So, I learned organically, and that was difficult because I had to trust Spirit, my integrity, and my body. But at the same time, it was very exciting.

I always thought my own personal healing was about learning to trust my intuition, and also to trust my reality, my goodness, and intention. That's how Spirit worked with me. I began to learn that what's important is my mind and also my body; my physical form. Years later I began teaching classes on developing one's own healing gifts, and the main thing that I hope to instill in my students is for them to be fully engaged in their physical form and to communicate and love their body. ***Be in your body, every single cell of it.***

What I've observed sometimes in the spiritual community is that some people are giving more value and attention to their higher vibrational self. But I believe your body needs you to be in it. For me it's that simple. I hear about people who work hard to be in the violet light, and to know the names of their guides, and so on. To me those things are not that important. We all have a huge family of angels and guides helping us. I believe it's more important to love yourself and your body, to listen to your spiritual heart and your intuition. It's important to have an intimate relationship with Creator and the Earth, and to have compassion for the people in our lives.

Back in the early '90s, as I continued to learn to meditate and trust myself, I had a couple of practitioners who affirmed what was happening to me, and what was happening when I touched people. This was at a time when I began getting spontaneous images of things inside a person's body. A friend called me one day and she started to tell me that she hurt her ankle, and as soon as she started talking about it, I saw in my mind's eye, an x-ray of her ankle and all the bones, and I could see which one was out of alignment. I was astonished. Another time I was talking on the phone about a man I had never met before, and without me trying, Spirit gave me a picture of his intestines and showed me exactly where he had a growth. Two days later, I found out that this man had an x-ray and his cancer was exactly as I was shown. I slowly accepted the fact that I had a gift and that I could help people.

Over the years, I began to offer medical intuition readings at health fairs. I don't look for any specific problems when I do a reading, Spirit shows me what is appropriate for me to see and talk about with the person at the time and I give the person the information. People have reported that it has saved lives. Some people have had profound emotional experiences when asked about a long, forgotten trauma. ***The body is a memory repository for everything we have experienced; everything.***

One time I was doing a medical intuitive scan on a woman and I saw something that looked like a little pearl on her genitalia and I told her exactly that. She wasn't aware of it. I reminded her that I do not diagnose but I suggested she might want to get it checked out. A year later, her daughter told me she was extremely grateful for the reading. She said that after her mother had the reading with me, she went to the doctor and found out that what I had seen was a very rare and aggressive form of cancer. She said that if her mother had not gone to the doctor at that time, she probably wouldn't have lived.

This is how I would explain how the medical intuition piece works. I always ask the person for permission to scan. I say a prayer and an intention before I start, that the information is accurate and appropriate for me to share with them. It seems my body is like a radar screen and the person's body communicates with my body. I see and/or feel things, and sometimes I get images that are anatomically correct, but more often than not, the images I get are metaphors for what's going on. Sometimes there is a strong emotional component to it, and that lets me know what I'm supposed to bring up, even if I don't understand it. I am extremely cautious and always share what I see or feel in the form of a question. Their body will give me a message that is appropriate for me to discuss with that person at that time. Sometimes I just get a little and sometimes I get a lot of information, and I just trust it. I don't go into every section of the body and scan every organ system like a snoop. I trust in the person's guidance system and whatever comes up, I share. We go as far as they want to go with it and what I am comfortable with. When it's appropriate, I offer some healing energy which involves transferring energy from the Universe into a person via a hands-on approach or from a distance. It all depends on the person, what they want, and what their mind and body are comfortable with. If it feels right, I suggest that they have whatever issue that comes up checked out by a doctor or therapist.

A lot of times people will open up and there will be a lot of tears during the reading, which can become part of the healing process. I am always surprised at how many people tell me they have not talked to anyone before about whatever issue it is that comes up for them. I find that one of the most healing things we can offer: someone with a compassionate ear.

I have noticed that all Medical Intuitives work differently. They have their own shtick because everybody is different.

When someone comes to my home for a healing session, we go to my healing room for the last part of the session. That part involves what I would loosely call shamanic journeying. Shamanism is about working with the invisible world, that's all it is. It involves work on one's spiritual and emotion heart. After my quick scan of the body, we call on their little child-self, the purest essence of who we are, to show up. I ask the client to communicate with their little child-self. This helps the person to get heart centered. I am not directing this, I am merely following the script that comes to me in that moment, as it naturally comes up on my spiritual screen.

I gently talk the person into a state where they go into their heart center, the heart chakra spiritual center, and I ask them questions. Again, I don't see what goes on with their body, I ask the person questions and they tell me what is happening. I guide them through this experience because they are not in their body now. I suggest they sit inside their spiritual heart and tell them to grow it bigger and bigger. I leave it to them as to how large they want it to be. I am holding the space and see none of this. That goes on for as long as need be for the healing in their body and based on what their little child-like self wants to do. To me, our child-like self is our true spiritual identity. Near the end, they travel back into their heart center which is home to their child-like self. I don't see it, but they tell me what happened when they grew their heart.

When they are back in their body, and ready, we talk about what happened. Many say things like, "My heart was bigger than the room, the house, then the earth," or "My heart was filling the whole universe!" We don't analyze it, I just tell them,

"That's wonderful," and ask how they felt then and now. They always say something like,

"I feel great!" They get to take that experience, those feelings of freedom and appreciation of self with them. I remind them that they can repeat this process anytime. They just journeyed outside of their body, and also deep into their spiritual heart center. It's a lovely gift that I am happy to offer.

I have a story which explains a little how this works. When I was around sixteen, I was really upset because I couldn't use the car and I ran upstairs to my bedroom and threw myself on my bed. I was heartbroken. I grew up Catholic and I really liked praying. I just went into this space as I was praying. All of a sudden, I left my body, and a second later, I went far beyond the solar system. I had a view of the whole earth and on some level, that I was too young to grasp at the time, I felt the Universe was taking care of me and everything else. What that experience said to me was, *Hey, listen, it isn't important.* That was the feeling that I got, and then I went back into my body.

I sat up in my bed and I felt a healthy sense of detachment from worldly worries. It gave me a grandiose perspective of life. Spirit had just pulled me out of my body, I wasn't trying to do it, and that amazed me.

Years later when I was in college my girlfriend and I were heading to a frat party, and I was telling my friend about this outer-body experience and she said, "Really, you can do that?" I said,

"Yeah, I've done it a few times."

"Can you do it right now?" I said,

"Sure, I can do it." I did it, and really it was just like stepping out into the cosmos again. It's kind of like rebooting, and I think it changed my vibration. We went to the frat party, and wouldn't you know, I got a date with the sexiest guy at the party! I wasn't deliberately trying to do anything different, but I think my vibration had changed and that changed the way I thought about myself.

The work that I do with medical intuition and the energy healing is all about energy.

I want to also mention that prayer is powerful, and the best prayer is said out loud so that all your cells hear your intention. When I pray for someone, I see them showered with love and peace. It is all about energy. It is my belief that we have an effect on anyone that we pray for.

I didn't take any classes to learn about the healing work that I do, but I kept getting messages and I had visitations from angels of all different types instructing me to just keep healing myself. As I healed myself, it was like a continuous spring cleaning, if you will, and new abilities would begin to surface.

I always remind people, though, don't look for most answers outside of yourself. Try to be clear about what's inside: the nonsense, the hurt, the sorrow, and the sense of not being good enough- all of that. Just keep going inward, which is the hardest thing to do. You can read books or go on week-long excursions or go to workshops, but you can also do a lot of powerful work by just sitting in your living room with meditation and prayer and asking for guidance.

I believe too often we have disengaged from the physical world; the third dimension, which is where we're supposed to be functioning. We came into this life in physical form for a reason, which is to walk around in this most familiar of dimensions and learn things, to enjoy this planet and to enjoy our lives and the connections with other people. Spiritualism does pull many people out of their bodies and it can become an addiction and, I wonder, maybe even an escape.

If someone came to me for a healing session, I would explain to them ahead of time that I offer the energy work and the medical intuitive scan, and then we usually start with a conversation. As the person is talking, their body is giving off information that cues me what to ask them. It's something like being a counselor, but I am listening intuitively to their body, then asking them questions after their body "says," *ask this*, and *ask that*, and we go from there.

Sometimes a person will want a past life scan. I don't do past life regressions which is different. What I do is similar to my medical intuitive scan. I put it out there energetically to my angels and to the person's guides, and I pray ahead of time that everything that happens is appropriate including everything I say and do. As I am doing the past life scan there is a communication that is happening between their highest guides and angels and my highest guides and angels and I get to listen in, ha, ha.

I start my scan with the crown chakra, and as I move my way down through the other chakras, the imagery will begin to show up. Sometimes it's like a mini dream, or a feeling I get, related to an image, and I share it with the person and ask them what it means to them. I might ask them what they think or how it makes them feel. That way, I am following their lead of how deeply they want to go into something. Sometimes when I am at a health or psychic fair, people completely shut down and I know they're not taking anything in and so not ready to learn, which is fine. For some people, the experience can be pretty profound, and can open up a door that they didn't even know was there. It can be related to either a very pressing and long-standing emotional memory, or it could be related to another life-time where there was great loss, trauma, or joy. The trauma is always carried into this life time. If the person requests it, I direct them to people who can help.

I offer thirty-minute workshops at fairs to introduce my past life readings and I offer mini readings in front of the workshop audience. Sometimes it's pretty humorous and we laugh because the reading is totally opposite of the person's personality in this lifetime. For example, one time while reading a man and his wife, I could tell that they were very, very conservative. I did a scan on the man and we were talking about the reading in front of everybody and it turned out that the man was a female prostitute in his past life. He and his wife were shocked! It has that kind of edginess that oftentimes people need, and it's like an invitation to expand one's thinking sometimes. Often the material that comes up is related to an ongoing relationship issue that a person might be having with their partner or family member or friend, or emotional issues with fear around something, or around some trauma that they had in another lifetime. I always share what I see and ask them one or two questions.

If it's a longer private reading and they have the need, I often suggest that they find a good counselor or get bodywork. Traumatic and or confusing past life experiences can cause problems with a person's energy, physical health, and or emotional health. I always encourage people to continue working on that memory with someone. Readings can be an emotional springboard to help a person go in a better direction or to get on with their lives.

At this point in the interview with Regina, she gave me the following past life reading:

They are showing me a vision of you dressed in white fur, and this may be metaphorical, but you are wearing a matching white fur hat, which has silver tips on it like mink fur. You are very fashionable, but you have a purse which you are a little frustrated with because someone gave you the wrong purse that didn't match your outfit. In this scene, you appear to be a model back in the era of the 1930s. You are on a stage for some type of commercial or promotion. Your face is quite beautiful, and you have ruby red lips. What I'm getting is that you were raised in a situation where you really didn't feel of value, but because of your beauty, you ended up in this position where people are looking at you. However, you know it is false, and you feel sad that people really didn't want to look beneath your beauty to get to know you. But you are okay with this because you wanted attention, and you finally got it. However, it won't lead to your emotional growth.

Very interesting. This past life reading took me by surprise, and as I wondered about whatever meaning it had, Regina told me that you can flip it around and sometimes with a former life we take on the roles of something opposite than we are working on in this lifetime. I have always been super camera shy all my life, and do not consider myself to be photogenic at all. I do not like being the center of attention. Is it because I had too much camera time in that past life? I have also always been very self- conscious, which is an issue I am always working on. Fortunately, I do have strong relationships with my husband, family, friends, and thankfully at this time in my life, I feel valued by those who love me.

I think that as each of us grows spiritually in our lifetime, the universe grows, and as each of us evolves, the universe evolves. We are supposed to do the best we can and give people help if they need it and not be overly judgmental.

I have twenty-five acres on my property at Forest Circles. It's very beautiful and very magical, which is an understatement. One of the things that I offer is that people can arrange for time to come out and spend time healing in the forest. In the past, people have brought a tent and spent the night or two or three, and I've had people come out and just sit under a tree for three days. I had a woman come out one time who just wanted to stay and sleep on the moss. I offer people a chance to go out in the forest and take stock of their lives and time and again they have amazing experiences.

I moved out here and had my house built in 2005, and I have a space where I offer healing sessions and I also host healers and teachers offering a great variety of cultural, spiritual traditions. I was guided to find this place by using my heart compass, and it is magical land which I love to share.

I try to teach people the value of going out into the woods and doing nothing. I believe it is a powerful medicine. If you can find a place in the woods, or anywhere in nature, just be still and don't do anything. Everyone is different, but for me it's like there's a potential to have an overlapping and melding of the earth's energy and mine. If you can clear your mind of its clutter by maybe focusing on an ant, a pine needle or a tree, that is what can happen, and it's pretty wonderful. **Don't work at doing nothing. Just stop.**

I would like to leave you with this wisdom. I always tried to impress upon my students that you must be in your body. Be fully engaged in your physical form. I always ask my students, where are you right now? Know where you are. Are you in your head, or are you in your heart, your spiritual compass? Are you in your own flesh and bones- kinds of places? Know where you're at. Have a full body experience, every day, all of the time. Be fully engaged in your body. If you can do that, I believe you will grow spiritually in the best of ways. Similarly, listen to the earth, for She knows things and She knows you.

To contact Regina for a healing or workshop, please call 207-776-3152 or email: rstrongheart@gmail.com.

Chapter 12

Cynthia Swan - Mystic
Priestess of the Temple of the Feminine Divine

Cynthia Swan was highly recommended by another mystic featured in this book because of her engaging personality, unique offerings, and pagan lifestyle, which were incredibly interesting to learn about. I had a wonderfully magical experience talking with her, and I gained some new techniques for healing and manifesting. Cynthia is an extraordinary astrologer, energy healer, mystic, and author who offers soul readings and astrological consults through her website, wickedgoodsoul.com.

I am an ordained Priestess of the Temple of the Feminine Divine which was started by Kay Gardner, who is also an amazing pioneer in music therapy. The Temple, which embraces and teaches "earth-based spirituality," consists of pagan clergy who have successfully completed the three-year program, leading to ordination. I am ordained through this temple, which is licensed as a church in Maine, and I can legally perform marriages in the state.

I was raised in a Catholic family, but like many Catholics, as I evolved and came into contact with other religions and other belief systems, I found that I gravitated toward a more earth-based spirituality. For me, paganism became my path in 1993 when I came into contact with a woman who was a Reiki practitioner and shamanic practitioner. She introduced me to Native American Spirituality when I went with her to my first intertribal Powwow, in Clinton, Maine. My intention at the Pow-Wow was to be a spectator, as I had no intention to participate in the Powwow, but there was one young Native American boy who insisted on pulling me out to dance a particular communal dance, and he wouldn't take no for an answer! Dancing with the group really spoke to my soul and I felt totally connected to the group and the earth in those moments. I remembered thinking, *"I am not Native American; I can't do this."* Once I started dancing in the circle with the group, I continued to dance during my entire stay at the Pow-Wow. I had two profound visions when I got home later that night after this life altering event. These were the first visions I have ever remembered having in my adulthood.

When you are a seeker, things you seek find you. I imagine it happens to all of us. That's how I met my Reiki teacher, who also had a Wiccan background. As I learned more, I connected with this earth-based reality. I was impressed by the idea that indigenous cultures honored Mother Earth, and that is what led me down the road to the Temple of the Feminine Divine. The program was a big commitment for me at the time, but I was able to embrace it, despite doubting my path periodically through this program.

Were you aware that you had spiritual gifts at all before this happened?

I had some unusual experiences as a child, but I was very steeped in Catholicism. Yet, I always had difficulty understanding how people around me could have this belief system, and yet they weren't living it in everyday life.

When I was about nine years old, I lived outside of Chicago and attended a Catholic school. During the religion class the nun, who was the instructor, said that anyone who was not Catholic was going to burn in hell. I was a mother's helper to a family who were Lutheran and had three young children, and I loved this family tremendously. That whole day I was on edge because I was anxious to tell the children's mother that they needed to become Catholic, or they were going to go to hell. I literally ran to her house after school and pounded on her door screaming because I had held it in all day. When she answered the door she said, "Cindy what is the matter?" I was terrified and could not stop sobbing as I told her,

"You have to become Catholic or you're going to go to hell." She grabbed my hands and said,

"Cindy, look at me. Do you really think that God, the God that you know and love, would send us all to hell, just because we don't believe the same way you believe?" Suddenly, although I was just nine years old, the light bulb went on and I'll never forget that moment. I looked up at her and said,

"No, He wouldn't do that. You are right."

That is when I started to really take a closer look at Christianity, the Jewish faith, and other organized religions. I realized that I was never going to find a religion that fit me because they are all driven by people, and people aren't perfect, therefore, in my belief, it became that no religion was perfect.

Nearly a decade after I had my spiritual awakening at the Powwow with the Native Americans, I found a clergy program on paganism, and I knew that was for me. Prior to that, I started practicing on my own, telling no one. I did my own rituals, I spent time outside, I read voraciously, and yet I told no one. I was completely in the closet until later in life, because I worked in a hospital in a very conservative environment. All that time I was reading tarot cards and doing numerology and astrology. I didn't come out of the closet publicly as Pagan until 2021 when I launched my online business, Wicked Good Soul LLC, because I just didn't want to deal with the whole "witch hunt" mentality and didn't want to hurt my family in any way. Prior to that, my closest and besties knew, but not everyone.

My life also changed dramatically when I was diagnosed with thyroid cancer in 2010. I worked very hard to keep half of my thyroid. Initially the surgeon told me I had to have it totally removed due to the cancer as that was the protocol. I choose to do the holistic route first, instead of rushing to surgery. At that point I decided that I was not going to let anyone else chart my course of life. Why I felt so strongly about this I just don't know, but at that time, I was internally driven by a passion to be true to myself. I wanted to go directly to the Divine. I was determined that if people wanted to judge me on that, then let them, because it's not my business what people think of me and I have no control over that anyway. I did a myriad of things and I believe it worked in my favor.

That is how the pagan clergy part of my life came about, the timing was right and I was ready to embrace my true destiny. I was ordained as a part of the class of 2013. Yet, in the beginning, I often questioned if it was the right way for me, but at one point when I was about to be ordained, I had an amazing dream which validated everything. I dreamed that I was in a hallway and I was opening all the doors, and suddenly, behind me, a door opened up on its own and there was a big black woman standing there. She told me to come in. I went into the room and there was a huge egg-shaped bathtub. She said, "Come here, come here," like a mother would say to her child. I went into her arms and she morphed into a gigantic, beautiful black bear. I wasn't afraid, and I remember feeling like I was home, and that this was where I belonged. The bear, by the way, is also one of many totems for the Goddess.

Since our earliest days, in the Paleolithic and Neolithic times, according to the histories and myths of the time, people have revered the earth, and therefore spirituality was earth-based. The Indigenous peoples revered the earth because that is what sustained them. They knew about seasons and the cycles. They knew the animals were gifts from the Divine, and where and when to hunt them. They had to be aware of how to grow their food, what to put away, what seed to keep, to store, and so on. The earth was the Mother, the nurturer, the provider.

I've always been a spiritual person, I just never wore it on the outside, ever. I have met people who seemed very spiritual, but their behavior did not match. That has always been a big bone of contention for me, so I never really talked about it. I tried to live it, and I was not trying to be perfect because no one is perfect. That is what I liked about paganism. There is no shame and you don't have to earn the badge to get to heaven. It is not a fear-based religion. It really is about the fact that there is a love for the Divine, for the Goddess, and a love for the earth. In our tradition we see the earth as a sacred, sentient being.

I put up a post recently on my website which said, "Witches are like ice cream, we come in all flavors." No two witches are going to agree on everything all the time, because we all have a different personal experience of the Divine. It is this diversity that I love so much about the Temple and that I love about the pagan pantheon, (all goddesses and gods). Everyone has direct communication to the Divine, and no one needs an intermediary. This really speaks to me.

Witches in my tradition, as in many others, honor the seasons as they cycle. We engage in rituals to celebrate specific holy days or Sabbats. We call this the **Wheel of the Year** and you will notice that these Sabbats have been absorbed into the Christian holy days. **Yule** is the Winter Solstice, the birth of the Sun, in Christianity it is the birth of the son of God. **Imbolc** is February 1st, the days are getting longer and the sun is warmer, spring is on its way. This is a time for spring cleaning and many pagans celebrate the Celtic goddess Brigid known for healing, poetry and smithing. The Spring Equinox ushers in **Ostara**, a name of the spring Saxon goddess who is associated with eggs, fertility, rabbits, you get the idea. Next up is **Beltane** on May 1st, ah, the lusty month of May, as the maypole is a phallic symbol that dancers weave around to celebrate this time of fertility on the land. Midsummer ushers in the Summer Solstice, **Litha,** the high point of the solar year, as at dawn it is the longest day of the year. **Lughnasa,** sometimes spelled **Lughnasadh** and also known as **Lammas,** is a harvest festival during which we enjoy gathering produce from the land and our gardens on August 1st. The Autumnal Equinox is known as **Mabon** and this is another time of harvest, Pagans will often refer to it as the Pagan Thanksgiving. With the ending of summer comes **Samhain**, aka Halloween, celebrating the end of summer and the beginning of the dark time as the daylight continues to wane and the landscape changes as the leaves fall from the trees. Thus, you have the eight Sabbats. Once Yule arrives the cycle repeats, never ending.

You also asked me about my work. I now offer what I call "Soul Readings," which include a number of modalities that I work with, including Aura-Soma. Aura-Soma is an esoteric system that incorporates color therapy, the chakras, astrology, and numerology. It also embraces the tarot and the tree of life, and you can bring in other esoteric aspects to it also. It's one of those esoteric systems that continues to grow tend develop, and so I use all of these tools from my metaphysical tool kit to give a reading. To begin, I have the person pick four out of several bottles, but in those four bottles lies their story, (what is going on in this cycle of time for them.) It's hard to explain, and you truly have to experience it. I tell people who don't have the time or money to book a reading with me to go online and look up Aura-Soma, pick four bottles and just read what those bottles say about you. It's a canned reading, but is no different than somebody jumping on and reading a daily horoscope. It offers some information and for some this shallow dip is enough for them.

I opened a part-time business in 2002, offering holistic therapies in conjunction with my day job at the hospital where I worked for seventeen years. Early on, I met an Ayurveda practitioner who came to my place to do a workshop on mantras. She was the one who introduced me to Aura-Soma. I loved it and I pursued it. It had all the esoteric things that I love: tarot, the colors, the numbers, aromatherapy, reincarnation and the chakras.

For a number of years, I was a radio host on WERU on an Integrative Medicine program I created called, Healthy Options. It is still running, and I am proud of having started it. It was to explore integrative medicine and I interviewed many people in Maine and outside of Maine. It was so easy for me, because I wasn't in the hot seat being peppered with questions. I was the one asking the questions. I did that show for well over seventeen years and I learned so much from these integrative professionals and healthcare providers. Having them on my show was just amazing and I loved being able to ask these providers questions about their passion and what they could offer to interested listeners. For example, we can learn so much from our just herbal community alone. Herbalists have a wealth of information.

You mentioned earlier that as a pagan person you are also a ritualist. What does that mean?

I think most people engage in ritual without realizing it. For instance, people celebrate birthdays. That's a ritual. People celebrate Thanksgiving, and they have their rituals of serving turkey, grandma's special rolls, pies, etc., whether it's with food, song, or dance, we all have our own unique rituals. As a ritualist though, what I'm talking about is that around each of the pagan holy days, the new moons and the full moons, I conduct solitary rituals. Periodically I am on Zoom, as a point priestess for the

Temple of the Feminine Divine, conducting public rituals for our Sabbats.

I believe rituals are in everybody's DNA, and that even as ancient souls, we all have some aspect of ritual in our lives. Ritual for me, is to set aside time to make a connection with Spirit for whatever the ritual is about. It may be about being thankful, or an inquiry for help. I can ritualize my life. For example, some people pray before they go to bed every night and that becomes a ritual. For me, every morning when I get up, I take the dog outside, and I do a ritual where I say a mantra, Om Lokah Samastah Sukhino Bhavantu, "May all beings everywhere be happy and know peace." I repeat that mantra every morning as I walk the grounds around my home. The second part of my daily morning walking meditation is that I do a prayer, "All above me Goddess, all below me Goddess, all before me Goddess, all behind me Goddess, all around me Goddess, All within me Goddess. Blessed be the Goddess that resides in me, Blessed be the Goddess in ALL."

Throughout the day, I have rituals to remind me that I have that personal link to the Divine. I do a ritual every night, where I send healing to everybody. I mean literally all my clients and everybody I know, and all my Facebook friends. It gives me a deep level of love and connection, and it also supports me. I also have the understanding that we live in an energetic universe and we are all connected. And like Ram Dass said, "We are all just walking each other home." We are all connected within this web of consciousness.

I told Cynthia that I repeat several positive affirmations every morning as I start my day. The affirmations replace my worries, and it really helps set me up for a good day. I have different mantras such as, "I am healthy, I am happy," and "My life is filled with abundance and prosperity." Whatever I am worried about, I turn it into a positive statement and I repeat each affirmation three times. It is one of the best things I have learned from mystics, and I can't say enough about how much that has helped me. A medium specifically told me during a reading that I was manifesting around water, which made me laugh, because I do these daily positive affirmations while in the shower.

We are electric beings; we are the body electric, and what

is water? Water is a conductor of electricity. I have read we are sixty to eighty percent water, depending upon who one references. When there's lightning, they tell you to get out of the water. Our bodies are conductors, and as that water is flowing over you in the shower, you are an energetic conductor. The water is also working through you, and washing you clean. What you may consider doing at the end of your shower is turn the temperature to very cold and it will boost your immune system, and you can also envision any negativity being washed down the drain. I work at taking all my negative worries and turning them around into positive mantras. It is about raising one's vibration.

If you have been to a spiritualist church perhaps you will have noticed that before they do a séance or table tipping, they will have the person sing or clap their hands to raise the vibration, because that happy, higher level of energetics brings in the higher energetic spirits. Everything is talking to us all the time. It just depends where one is going to put their energy.

Some of the best teachings I have learned are from Paramahansa Yogananda, who wrote the book, *The Autobiography of a Yogi*, which is my favorite book in all the world. In one of his other books about the Divine, he talks about how to help yourself if you're feeling fearful, by placing your hand over your heart, and moving your hand from left to right over your heart, repeating a positive mantra over and over, while you breathe slowly. For example, if you are worried about a loved one you can say, "I know that all is well, and I know that the Divine protects my loved one." Repeat your mantra over and over and breathe through it until you feel a shift in energy and a calmness within. Remember that energy follows intention, so you can't do it wrong.

In traditional Asian medicine, the Conception meridian and the Governing meridian, which come up the spine both connect at your hard palate right behind your front teeth. Let's say you are at work, and something is upsetting you, but you can't do the hands on the heart practice. Try putting your tongue there behind your front teeth and breathing slowly through your nose. Do the deep breathing slowly, and it brings calm to the body. It's because you are connected to the main circuitry in the meridian system of your body. It is very powerful and it does work. All of these tools work, you just need to practice them.

You are so full of great information about energy and healing. I wish I could download all your wisdom into my understanding.

I live it. I love it! It's my life. When I worked in the hospital environment, I sometimes felt like I straddled two worlds. There is the spiritual world, then there's the mundane, and they are connected, but sometimes we aren't. You go to work and you experience people who complain, or you complain and are very negative. It can affect your energy system, and it's also hard when negative energy is bombarding us, or we ourselves are being negative. It's hard to divert it or let it go. We have to work with techniques that help us to release it. That's why even in my last Astrology Tik Tok episode I spoke about the full moon energy. I told people to be careful what you listen to. Be careful who you are around. Be careful who you speak to and how you speak because the energies are more ramped up than usual around that time. Just being aware of it is helpful. Astrology can help you be forewarned, and forearmed. It is a wonderful symbolic language that offers us information and guidance.

I have been following Donna Eden, an energy practitioner, for years and I find her work to be very helpful for me especially when I worked in the hospital setting. I believe every hospital has at least three angels overlooking and overseeing it all the time, because there can be so much negativity and trauma there. So, when I went to work at the hospital I would do her "Zip up." The "Zip Up" is that you go to the area of your pubic bone and you envision the bottom of a zipper and you pull the zipper up to your top lip. As you are zipping up, you say, "I am zipping up and I am protecting my energy field, so that I am safe and protected no matter what is around me." It's like putting on your winter coat when it's freezing out. It is from her book, *Energy Medicine.* Her work is phenomenal, and all of these exercises are on her YouTube and they are free.

I asked Cynthia to explain how it works when people go to her for a soul reading.

I have my own spiritual tool box, ritual, and prayers which I do before a reading. I let people know that this is a Divine consultation between you and me. You're not dependent upon anything I tell you, you are dependent upon your own "knowing," and that is what I want to reflect in a reading. I want to reflect your soul's knowledge and your Divinity. I have several tools and I can't use them all as it would be overwhelming for the person, but I know that I am guided. I can feel it. When I do the reading, and I am looking at the bottles, I am reading what I have learned; the brain part of the learning. But when I'm reading someone and I'm looking at the bottles, it's hard to explain, but it's like a light goes on when I am guided. As I am talking to the client, I will say something like, "Oh and with your anxiety, this may help you." Or, "I see turquoise in your bottle and that indicates energy medicine might be a fit for you."

I might be talking to someone who is going through a health crisis and they tell me they have been going to a doctor but not getting any better, so I might ask if they have tried a Reiki treatment. I may suggest choices that might be helpful to them based upon their astrological chart or Aura-Soma choice. They may be a candidate for some type of energetic work that could compliment what their doctor is doing. I may suggest they ask their doctor if it's okay and if the doctor says it's okay to do, and if they've got the finances to do it, then give it a try. If a person doesn't have the money, I tell them what to look for online, so they can plug-in and try things at no monetary cost, and perhaps they can access what they need.

I say on my website that the readings are ninety minutes, but they usually last a full two hours to be honest, because we go deep. I want people who are willing to really go deep and do the work. This is my calling. This is how I have to be authentic. The online readings work well and people love it because they are at home and relaxed, and they can be all snuggled in with their pajamas on and with a cup of tea. I recommend that people record the entire reading. It is a very in-depth connection, so it doesn't matter if we are on Zoom, because we are still connected energetically. I find that it is one of the advantages of the Aquarian age of technology, and it makes me more available to help people. It was the pandemic that got me to launch my online platforms.

Most people don't come to me for a reading when their life is going great. They hire me when they are at a critical juncture, or when they are confused, or troubled. What I say to everybody is that because of the Aquarian Age we are entering, we are all going through a time of change. This is one of those things that is preordained. We are going through a massive change universally. Yes, it is very chaotic and divided and divisive right now. We are all going through this together, although with different experiences of this quality of time, and hopefully as we get to the other side, we will be better for it. We will see a better, more loving community and more Aquarian; living the higher octave. We are heading towards a more humanitarian way. Community is Currency! This is a great opportunity because it is when humans are uncomfortable that they look at themselves and wake up and they say, *what are we doing?* Kind of like when a person goes to therapy and they need it very badly. They usually wait until it is really terrible and they can't stand it anymore, and that's when they want change and they reach out for help or call a counselor.

I believe we are coming to a time where people are going to have to reach out to their neighbor for help and for things they need, even essentials like food or toilet paper. We will have to rebuild our communities by helping each other out and sharing what we each have to share. The whole world is going through a crazy time, and it's not over, and it won't be quick, because I believe as we astrologers have talked about, it will be 2024 or 2025 before we see some of the necessary changes solidified or at least indoctrinated. This is still unfolding and we are in the unfolding.

Blessed Be.

For more information about Cynthia or to contact her for a soul reading or astrological consult, her website is: wickedgoodsoul.com.

Chapter 13

Vicki Laflin - Crystal Bowl Meditations
and Alchemical Healing

I have known Vicki since we were children, but I didn't know about her healing abilities until a few years ago and only recently realized the extent of her remarkable gifts. I was aware that Vicki was a Master Reiki Healer, but I wasn't very knowledgeable about any of the energy healing modalities which she had been practicing for years, and even life times. Vicki tends to keep to herself about her spiritual gifts for reasons which she explains later.

I began participating in Vicki's Crystal Bowl meditations a few years ago, which are offered monthly. These meditation sessions provide sound healing in a wonderfully relaxing way. Vicki "plays" several beautiful crystal bowls of different sizes by rubbing around the edges with a soft mallet, each bowl producing different tones which resonate with each of the chakra energy centers. Crystals have been known for thousands of years for their powerful healing qualities and they are also able to increase a person's vibrational energy. The musical tones of the crystal bowls create vibrations which break up energetic blockages and clear the chakra centers.

A Crystal Bowl Meditation is a very enjoyable experience, and people report everything from feeling deeply relaxed, to seeing colors, to astral travelling. It is a unique healing modality.

On one memorable summer evening I attended a full moon crystal bowl meditation with Vicki in a large barn in Mount Vernon, which belonged to her friends. As we all sat on cushions or lay on mats on the floor of the restored barn, looking up at the rafters above decorated with tiny white lights, the tone of the crystal bowls had an ethereal effect. Afterwards, the group of spiritual minded friends gathered around a bonfire for an enchanted evening and shared their experiences.

In addition to full moons, Vicki offers crystal bowl meditations during spring and fall equinoxes, which intensifies the effect of the experience. She offers meditations in her home and she will also travel and do groups if requested.

Vicki is a Reiki Master Practitioner, Master Level Integrated Energy Therapist, Herbalist, and Shamanistic Healer. She is knowledgeable about everything from energy healing to understanding and experiencing mysterious realms such as those of spirits, angels, fairies, and other elementals.

I recently learned that Vicki is also an Alchemical Healer, and asked her to explain this ancient healing method which dates back to the Egyptian times.

A Healer is someone who helps you to find the key within you, for your own ability to heal. I began my learning about alchemical healing when I was drawn to a book on a shelf. As I perused it, I was struck by how it made so much sense to me. Later, I went out to Oregon and studied with Nicki Scully, an internationally known Shamanic healer, and author of the book, Alchemic Healing. Her alchemical healing program is not the same as other healing modalities because anything can come through with this healing from the spirit world, including your guides or angels. If something is important to you, it will come through. When you're lying on the massage table having a healing session, I sit beside you and talk with you and you're the one who discusses the healing with me, as I am doing the healing with you. For example, if you have a fear of lions, a lion may come in and sit under the table, so that you can feel that vibration or get over that feeling. Your loved ones who have passed, your spirit guides, and your angels may come through during the session. Sometimes, I may intuitively use crystals or plant energy, because the vibration of a certain plant might be what your body needs for healing. We can use the energy of fire, the earth, water, or air. It's not just a touch healing, I am drawn to help shift your energies while you are awake and consciously participating. During the session, I may tell you what I'm seeing and ask how it makes you feel, or ask what it may bring up for you.

When people come in and lay down on the massage table, I usually have the client do what is called a Heart Breath, which is like a little mini-meditation that helps to center and ground and relax them. Next, I ask the person's guides and angels to assist in bringing in whatever is needed for healing, or for clearing. In the beginning, we discuss why the person is there, whether they are curious and just want to experience alchemic healing, or if there is a specific issue that the person wants to deal with. Most often, people come to me for physical pain or emotional issues. When we are born, we are pure energy and we vibrate at a perfectly balanced level. But once we start living in this reality, all kinds of issues can come in at any time that a person is out of balance energetically. That's when disease can come in. Stress and other issues can knock you off balance.

Most people associate alchemy as the process of turning lead into gold. With alchemical healing, it's changing the vibration and loosening the stuck energy and the 'stuff' that you no longer need, so that you can become the vibration that you should be. Integrated Energy Therapy, IET, works with the Angels and their much higher vibration on a cellular level. It is an extremely peaceful and loving vibration. However, with alchemical healing, the healing takes place on a molecular, vibrational level.

After the alchemical healing session, the person often experiences very profound shifts and changes. That healing continues to work on your body for twenty-four to forty-eight hours after the session. Things continue to shift, and once you get past that process, you may see new things happening and changing in your life.

To explain further, a person's soul and body are all vibration. Even physical things like a table or chair are energy, but denser and solidified. Everything is energy, and energy is always vibrating. When we are not vibrating properly, we are not in balance, and that's when issues come up. Disease is disease. There is something not functioning properly energetically. Everything has to do with energy, and it all goes back to energetic balance. For example, when I do crystal bowl meditations, the crystal bowls are about vibration and shaking up every cell in your body to a vibration level, so that everything that is stuck in your chakra centers are cleared, because blocked energy happens when they are not spinning properly.

I do not advertise my healing modalities as a rule, and instead have relied on word-of-mouth and recommendations from those I have healed. I feel that if people want to find me, they will be guided to me, or something will happen and they will be led to me. In several of my past lives I have been persecuted for being a healer and for doing the same kind of work over millennia. I have done this kind of healing work many, many times over many lives. I have always been a little guarded about my gifts. This has been a hurdle which I have had to work through in order to put myself out there and advertise what I do. It comes very hard for me. This is something that I have done for many, many lifetimes, so I bring a lot of different aspects of healing to my work. I think that is why I was drawn to the alchemical healing work, because it encompasses so many different aspects of what I do.

In my Alchemical healing session with Vicki, I received a strong message about loving myself from my animal spirit guide. I had heard about my brown bear guide before from another medium, and I was told that my bear is always with me, protecting me and giving me strength and courage. When Vicki first mentioned that a brown bear came in to the session, I was quite impressed.

After using tones from bells which Vicki played over my body to break up and move stuck energy with the vibrations, Vicki guided me with a visual meditation. As I lay on the massage table in a mystically decorated, warm room in her home, Vicki described earth energy coming up through my feet, legs and body to ignite a flame in my heart, and also simultaneously ethereal energy from above coming down through my crown chakra, through my neck and chest to my heart. When Vicki told me that the brown bear who came into the room, (I did not see it, but I felt a warm trust in what Vicki was describing as she sat by my side,) the feeling was very powerful and surreal. I was amazed as Vicki described my brown bear guide as it walked around me, sniffing me and then energetically making an incision with its claw above my heart. The bear then took my heart out and held it in the air and then dug a place in the earth to lay it upon. He then walked into the woods and gathered herbs which he placed in the cavity where my heart was, to fertilize and repair what Vicki said was my heart needing healing. I just laid there very relaxed and astonished by the whole thing. It was very beautiful. The bear gently placed my heart back in my body, packing it with the herbs and then crawled on top of me with all four legs around me, giving me a huge bear hug. Vicki said that the bear wanted me to know it was important to love myself. It was incredibly wonderful to experience as I listened to Vicki's guidance and observations.

Archangel Michael came through next and stood at my feet, then cut many energetic cords which were holding me back from being my happiest self. I call upon Archangel Michael often, and so was not surprised that he came through for me in this healing session. The cord cutting was very powerful to experience as well. Tears rolled down my cheeks the entire time.

Next, Vicki saw Daisy, my yellow lab who passed away two years ago. She said Daisy came into the session to let me know that she was still with me and still walked beside me when I hike in the woods. It was wonderful to hear and to imagine her there.

My experience with the alchemical healing was subtle but wonderful, and I trusted that the healing of my heart and the energetic cord cutting had the ability to bring future changes and open new energy in my life. It was just a beautiful experience. Vicki assured me that in each healing session, a person gets exactly what they need unlocked and unblocked for healing for that time, as we are all learning and growing as evolving souls on this earth. I highly recommend Vicki for any healing session she offers.

To contact Vicki to set up a Crystal Bowl mediation, Reiki, IET, or Alchemical Healing, email her at: harmonyhavenhealings@myfairpoint.net or 207-320-8448.

Chapter 14

Jeanie Sullivan-Psychic Intuitive
Heartfelt Energies

Jeannie Sullivan is a remarkable psychic intuitive, and the founder/owner of Heartfelt Energies, which is a spiritual/ metaphysical business based in Hallowell, Maine. When doing readings, she uses tarot cards to begin the process, but reads very intuitively, allowing more than just the cards into a reading. Often times loved ones, spirit guides, angels, and animals join in on the conversation.

I have been an empath my entire life, which helps me to read and feel energy. I have the ability to not only feel my own energy, but other's as well. This helps to make me a really great healer with strong healing abilities. I've always been able to read people and situations in some form or fashion my entire life.

Ten years ago, I decided to become a Reiki Practitioner and open my own practice. I became attuned to Reiki and with time became a Reiki Master/Teacher. I also became familiar with an energy modality known as Primus Activation Healing Technique and became attuned to this as well. Primus is an energy modality that works with the Earth's electromagnetic field to balance, ground, and center you. It is fantastic for emotional, as well as physical issues. It is a modality that I love because it helps the client to feel as though he/she has had a massage for their soul.

As my spirituality grew and I became introduced to other practices that included shamanism, I fell in love with this energy and what I was learning. It felt to me as though I had found my home. I completed a Medicine Wheel class and, as a result, became a Mesa Carrier. The mesa I created was a healing Mesa. In short, it's a bunch of stones that I put my heart, soul, tears and sweat into. It was an inexpensive way to go into intensive therapy for a year, and I learned so much about myself. As they say, "healer heal thyself," and the medicine wheel process did that for me in a very big way.

The mesa I created includes practices that come from the Toltec traditions in Peru. Many indigenous cultures use mesas for a variety of reasons. Each culture incorporates their own traditions and archetypes into creating a mesa. My mesa consists of thirteen stones wrapped in a sacred cloth. It took a year to complete the exercises and training. I worked very closely with the four directions and each of the archetypes that represent the south, west, north, and east. I did a variety of lessons for each direction that included using stones to represent various aspects of the mesa. Because my mesa happens to be a healing mesa, I incorporate it into the energy sessions I do for clients. It is always in the room when I do Reiki or Primus sessions.

All the modalities I have learned, allow me to offer a wonderful experience for my clients. I would describe my healing sessions that I do for people as a wonderful mix of energy with indigenous energy being at the forefront of my sessions.

Shamanic healing comes from a very earth based indigenous culture. Shamanism is not necessarily Native American, but any indigenous culture from around the world. My training includes Peruvian Toltec practices, so I follow those traditions, which I sometimes feel a little funny doing, because I am a glow-in-the-dark white American woman.

I try very hard not to steal their culture or ways. I consider myself a guest in this culture and treat it with great respect. I call myself a shamanic practitioner, not a shaman, out of respect, as I am not native to the ways of what I have studied. My teachers have taught me in the Peruvian Toltec tradition, so that has different aspects to it than Native American, Celtic, or aboriginal shamanism.

As I have grown, changed and become more confident in myself and my abilities, both my energy sessions and readings have changed over the years. When I first started doing psychic readings, I used cards exclusively, but as time went by, other senses have come into play. Now not only can I read and feel spirits, but they now leave me smells, sounds, and sometimes tastes. It all sounds exciting, but sometimes taste is my least favorite. For a variety of reasons, the tastes they leave me are not always pleasant. Fortunately, this does not happen too often.

Now when I use tarot cards, I use them very intuitively; it is a jumping off point for me, that kind of "primes the pump" and gives the person being read something pretty to look at. In the beginning I relied on the actual meaning of the tarot cards. As my energy and intuition has shifted and changed, what I have learned, and what Spirit has shown me, has conformed my readings to go way beyond simply telling the story of tarot. I have always had a direct connection to Spirit. My readings have changed to a much richer and stronger intuitive reading. Other beings come into the reading like loved ones, spirit guides, and angels, so it goes beyond tarot.

It was not easy growing up as an empath. My family was dysfunctional, and growing up we did not talk about feelings or anything else for that matter. I really didn't know what I was for a very long time. It wasn't until I was grown and started taking classes on what an empath was that I thought, "Oh, I am that!"

One of the hallmark things about being an empath is that people feel very comfortable around me, and often within five minutes of meeting me they may start telling me very personal things. As an empath, my energy feels good and so safe that people often blurt out personal things to me. So, growing up I just always knew that I was different, but I didn't know how or why, until later.

I have had abilities all of my life. I wouldn't change how I grew up, or who I had as parents and siblings. They have helped to shape who I am today. I often read for people who have had similar stories to my own. I feel that helps in having compassion, understanding, and empathy for my clients. I love what I do and have met amazing people along the way.

I scheduled a Primus energy healing session with Jeanie, and because of the Covid pandemic, she was able to give me healing distantly. She told me to sit quietly during the session at an appointed time in a comfortable place. She mentioned that some people experience her energy as feeling like light rain falling on their feet, and said she would call me back when she was finished to discuss the healing. She explained she was going to start at my feet and move up through my body to my head, then back down to the feet again. I chose to sit in my living room on the couch because the low November sun was shining in at a nice angle through the porch windows, which made me feel cozy. I put my feet up on the coffee table and my feet immediately felt tingly- but was it my imagination? I tried not to over think, and just relaxed and meditated. Thoughts came and went as I sat there comfortably, but mostly I felt happy and thankful for the connection to Spirit and the healing which I trusted was happening. I enjoyed every minute.

When Jeanie called me back, she said that she had some interesting experiences while doing my healing. She said she saw clear quartz crystals from the top of my hips all the way to the bottom of my feet. She said I was so completely full of the crystals that "they" had filled my hips and legs. She sensed there was an energy block and asked if I had arthritis or something at the top of my legs. I explained that I have osteoporosis in my hips and some arthritis in my ankles and feet.

She said when she first started working on my feet, my shins literally looked black, perhaps indicating blockages because the energy couldn't get through at first. Curiously, she saw a pair of old-fashioned winter boots, fur lined leather laced, beside my feet. She wasn't sure what that meant and wondered if the boots were there for protection. She said the crystals were bright, shiny, glowing and fun to watch.

She had to work for a while in my pelvic area too, she said, giving it more strength-especially my hips. She also described seeing my base chakra as very red and my sacral area bright orange, and that all of my chakras were vibrant and spinning, but she did have to work on my stomach area a bit.

She said when she got up to my head area a very pretty purple color came through-which is associated with the spiritual realms, and it infused my other chakra colors.

Jeanie described that when she worked on my heart chakra it was very bright green and when she gave it some Primus, it just drank the energy in like, "Ahhh, this is great"! (Interesting and likely no accident that Vicki Laflin recently did Alchemical healing on me and the focus was opening and healing my heart chakra-assisted by my bear guide-very interesting.) She added that I was fun to work on as I was in a really good place and welcoming to the energy and experience, and therefore open to the Primus energy, especially my heart, which seemed thirsty and just kept drinking and drinking in the energy. I believed and resonated with everything Jeanie said, and truly I enjoyed that hour tremendously and was extremely grateful for the experience. She said the energetic healing would continue to work, especially the crystals, until I didn't need it anymore, and to drink a lot of water all day to help the energy move through. I am very thankful for the opportunity to receive healing from Jeanie and highly recommend her for a reading or healing session.

Jeanie can be reached through her email: heartfeltenergies@gmail.com.

Chapter 15

Kathryn Drage-Animal Communication

I always thought that my beloved yellow lab, Daisy, had that look in her eyes, as if she understood exactly what I said when I talked to her. I later had a confirmation during a psychic reading that literally said that Daisy understood everything I said to her. A few years later I had a reading with another medium who described Daisy with accurate details and told me that (Daisy) wanted me to know that the reason we loved each other so much was that we had been together in another lifetime. I can't explain why, but I just knew that was true. Daisy was my "soul dog," and that reading helped me in the following years when her health began to fail as she grew old and when we had to say goodbye. I have received messages from Daisy in every reading I've had since that time. I know she is always with me.

During this interview I was impressed by Kathryn's extraordinary qualities, and I had to go very deep to absorb her words and profound wisdom with animal communication.

I Consider it a heartfelt responsibility when I do animal communication publicly. It is extremely important for me to find a place where humans can hear the message the animal brings to them in a heartfelt way, and with integrity and love. It is important to me that I honor the animal, that I am effective and reach people at a heart level.

With images of Dr. Doolittle in mind, I asked Kathryn what it's like to talk with animals.

It is not easy to explain, but when I hear an animal's voice, I may hear a different accent, or sometimes it's a stern voice, and sometimes it's a comical voice. That doesn't mean that's what it sounds like, but it puts me on the same wavelength as what they are trying to have me receive for information. The important thing is that 'knowing' piece. My intuitive, gut feelings are usually accompanied by an image, which might be seeing a single image, or it may be a whole scene playing through. I am able to see the story they are trying to show me. I want people to realize this is how we all can feel and interpret messages. Sometimes I push away thoughts that come into my head, thinking it's just my busy mind, but when I slow it down, I realize that even the cartoon characters that I frequently see are part of the message. This may not be how it happens to everybody, but I know I'm not the only one.

It is easier to illustrate through stories how I experience animal communication. A long time ago, I was offering animal communication readings at a pet food store. I was in the grooming room doing brief readings and towards the end of the day a mother and son came in. The son was about seventeen years old and he and his mother sat about four feet away from me. They were very hyperactive and they wanted to know why their dog was hyper. They were flinging questions at me and not waiting for the answers, so it was a little intimidating for me as this was my first time doing public readings like this. Their final question was, what was the name of their dog that passed away? I thought, oh my goodness, because whoever wants to come through will come through, and it is not always under my control. I closed my eyes and I asked the universe to help me. I kept on having an image of a sour cream container going through my head and I thought, *what is this?* It was a matter of not even a minute and I heard a little tune. I blurted out, "If I have to say anything, I would say her name is Daisy."

The son literally jumped up and his chair flew out behind him! I think they were trying to figure out if I was authentic. They've been clients of mine ever since, and if I told them the story, they would probably not even remember it. I had to learn that my quirky little visions are an important part of the message. I had never even purchased the Daisy brand of sour cream before, but that's an example of the way I see things.

I wondered if it was a coincidence that the first story which she chose to tell to me that day was about a dog named Daisy, as I was secretly hoping she might pick up on my Daisy as we talked. Later in the interview when I mentioned this, Kathryn said she wasn't sure why that story of all stories came up, and it was most certainly my Daisy saying hello!

I have another example of how animals give me messages. Once, I was doing a reading and I saw a vision of an old bulldog lounging on a beach holding a Margarita drink. I avoided telling the people exactly what I saw at first, but when I finally did, they shouted, "That's him!" Apparently, the dog never actually lounged on the beach holding a drink, but they said they spent a lot of time at the beach together. They often had happy hour on the beach near their home, and that's how they recognized their dog. I have learned to not push away these odd pictures or feelings because they are always an important part of the reading.

When I was in my mid-30s, I found a beautiful orange coon cat named Clem. I was going into an elevator -that's how I met him- and he traveled up to the third floor with me. I ended up bringing him home with me because I knew he was a stray cat. He came home with me and he literally woke me up and dragged me out of the animal communication closet. I didn't realize what I was sensing before that. He helped me recognize my gift, and he saved my life.

This cat Clem beautifully taught me wisdom that was profound. He told me that we have to think more positively. It is not just about what we say, but how we think, because what we think about holds huge value. Sometimes we don't even realize what kind of thoughts are cycling through our minds, and it may be worrying about circumstances, money, politics, or negative self-talk. Our animals respond to what's going on with us and often begin exhibiting acting out behaviors like shutting down, becoming ill, or urinating in inappropriate places. There are so many different things going on and it all starts with energy. If we are open to it and we look deeper at what we're thinking and doing, it will be healthier for us, as well as our animals. It is then that the healing can begin.

Animals are beautiful mirrors of our thoughts, behaviors, and the circumstances in our lives. There is so much more healing that can happen for us and the animals as well, when we pay attention to the messages. I can explain this best with the following story: A woman called me for assistance because her cat had suddenly started urinating everywhere in the house. She also mentioned that at the same time her husband got a new job and started travelling a lot. Every time the husband left, the cat peed someplace in the house. She said it was as if the cat was "pissed." Before I left my house that day, my own cat, named Butterfly, told me that the cat I was going to see looked just like her. Often my own cats will give me insights into animals I am going to read, because they are always in touch telepathically.

I went to the home and the family showed me a picture of the cat, because the cat had run off into the woods. This cat was almost identical to my cat, which made my level of love and empathy go even deeper, because of my love for my cat. So, this cat asked a question and I could hear this telepathically. At the same time her husband was pacing in the other room. Sometimes when people have me come to their homes, their spouse, or other family member, might not be on board with animal communication and the person often says, pay no attention to him. As the woman and I talked, I asked her some questions, and she had what we call an "ah ha" moment. She suddenly realized what was happening. She said she and her husband had been married for over twenty years, but both had been married previously. The woman's first husband was on the road a lot and he cheated on her. This cat was mirroring the woman's cellular memory. Every time her present husband went away, on an unconscious level, she became insecure. Her cat was mirroring her unconscious feeling of being insecure. I am always very amazed at the message that comes forth, and the healing as a result.

Another important thing is that when I am working with an animal, I often see words in my mind's eye, floating around the animals. A horse explained this to me years ago. He said that words are important affirmations, which become a part of the healing. Sometimes I see colors too, and sometimes I'll see a vegetable floating around them, which can indicate vitamins that their bodies need. When I see a word, it's always positive and always in the present tense, and the animal will mirror that. The words given help shift insecure feelings to secure. When I give the animal's companion a list of words to use as affirmations, the animal will mirror those words. When using these affirmations, it is important that the person focus on the feelings of the words.

Around the same time, I was learning about the importance of words from the horse, I had read about Dr. Masaru Emoto, who researched words and emotions and their effect on people and animals on a molecular level. During his experiments he discovered that positive and negative words had definite physical results. You can look him up and see videos that illustrate how this works, and it is fascinating.

Often when I see animals who have been rescued, the word or phrase which comes up for them is, "I am secure." You have to think about what the word or phrase means. We want them to feel secure in their own skin, and sometimes those are the words I see around them. If you stop and take a few seconds to think about what the word "secure" feels like in your body, the animal will start mirroring that. There was a whole different list of words that the cat had.

The woman later told me, "Don't let my husband fool you. After you left, he was the one holding the cat and saying the affirmations!" The woman also said that in the five years that the cat lived after that, she only peed in the house a few times, and it was when the woman said she forgot to check herself when her husband went off to work. You know it wasn't even a conscious thing for this woman at first, but it's an example of how animals know and mirror where their people are at. Animals are able to give beautiful messages to what's going on.

I want to explain more about words and thoughts and how they affect the mirroring process with animals. I learned something important from the cat Clem, who taught me something very significant about the words and thoughts that I had, not just at home, but at work and elsewhere. When I came home from work and had experienced a hard day, he was having a hard day too. I want to make clear that he was hit by a car or something before we met. He had injuries and I took him to my holistic vet and a chiropractor and it helped him. But I still noticed that when I was at work, and if I had a frustrating day and came home complaining about it, he would say, "Don't do this anymore. Think better and you will feel better."

I learned to rearrange my words to have things come out in a more positive way, which was noticeably better for him. I could be miles away from him and he still picked up on my thoughts. He showed me that when I go into people's homes, we have to be better, and think better. We have to look at ourselves because we have such a strong bond with our animal companions, and we influence each other. Ultimately the animals help us "up our game," so to speak. The animals mirror back and show us in a physical way what we are doing. When I was not checking myself and being negative, the cat started having a hard time walking again. I learned this coon cat had more declined physical health when I had more declined thoughts and behavior.

Another thing I want people to think about with words is not to refer to pets and their "owners." It is kinder and more energetically inviting to use the terms, "animal companion," and "human companion."

I am a better person after every animal communication session, because I learn about profound things that are beyond me. Animals are such beautiful beings, and they amaze me, every time.

Our animals love us unconditionally. It's the language they know. We hide nothing from them, and we are so unfiltered around them. I believe this is the reason that when people grieve over losing their animal companions, it is often, for many, more difficult than when they lose another human in their lives.

People have different beliefs on the topic of death, and I was shown by animals that they call it "crossing through," rather than "crossing over."' I know a lot of people think that there is an "in-between place," and people sometimes reach out to me because they are worried that their animal might be lost in the "in- between place." What I have been shown by animals is that most of the time the crossing is very quick, and also, they have their own spirit guides who help them cross through. Sometimes they say they just put on their "spirit suit," and sometimes a dog will show me that his mother was there when he crossed through. They show me there is a beautiful white and gold cocoon that they are wrapped in, and even though their body might be experiencing something critical, they are already on their way. The transition is most often very smooth and loving for them; that's what they talk about the most to me.

What I tell people is that their beloved is well and that they bring so much love. Sometimes people have guilt about the way things happened in the end. Often an animal doesn't show their people what's going on with them with their illness until they're ready for their people to see it. I can tell you that I find most of the time the animal tells me that they would never have lived as long if it wasn't that they loved their people so much and vice versa. Furthermore, that if it wasn't for that love, they would have given up and left a long time ago. Our power of love is huge and so is theirs, which is why there is so much healing. I want people to know that the number one thing is that love is the biggest, strongest, best medicine out there. Animals are so open and honest they will show you that it's working. It is amazing. This is why I gravitate towards them; because animals only tell the truth. They just show you. Animals are always open and honest.

When my cat Clem passed away, I was distraught and had guilt over it. He had helped me so much and he turned my world around. Looking back, it was as if I was not consciously aware before, and he is the reason I do animal communication. I asked him when he passed away what I could do for him because I was so upset, and he asked me to continue to do this in his honor. He said, "Don't let my life go in vain. Reach one heart and one being at a time."

It's the core reason that I do this, and my goal is to help both the animal and the human. It's about finding harmony in their lives together. It's all about the love, and looking at life through their perspective.

Before I began to do this publicly, I went online for information and I took classes on animal communication. I found a special book which influenced me very much, which is called, *A Kinship with all Life,* by Jay Allen Boone, who I believe was a great-nephew of Daniel Boone. This book, written in the 1950s, is about an experience that Jay had with this dog that he was caring for. The dog was actually the original White Fang, the biggest star in the 1930s. His name was Strongheart. Jay Allen Boone was a Hollywood writer, back when you could hike up in the hills. This dog taught Jay about animal communication. Jay never intended to go out and learn this, it is just what happened as a result of them being together. One of my biggest take-aways from this book came from a time when they were up on the heights sitting overlooking the sunset, which was what it looked like to others. The bigger picture was that here were two beings allowing the Universe to flow through them.

This is exactly what I believe in my heart about animal communication. That's how the profound spiritual messages come through, just as we are opening up to that level and letting it flow. That's why I say it's a language, and anyone can do this. It is energy work, which is an ego- less thing because when you're at that place, you're allowing it to flow through you.

Another important thing I want to share is that I don't call myself a healer. It is the being, person, or plant, etc., that I'm working with that does the healing. I am just offering a higher vibration, and their innate intelligence helps them do what they need to do in their body, and puts the healing where it is needed. I don't know where it is needed, but the inner intelligence of the being does. I am merely the facilitator offering a higher vibration, and their innate intelligence meets up with that. I find it very beautiful and that's where the honesty of animals comes through.

I also use what I call medical intuition with animals. The way it works is that I sense or feel what they are feeling. For example, sometimes I literally feel itchy if an animal has an allergy. I can tell that a dog has been over-vaccinated and has what is called vaccinosis, when I get a metal taste in my mouth comparable to a tin can. I had to discover these things along the way. The signs I get, help pinpoint what is going on with the animal that I am seeing, whether it's physical or emotional. One time, I was asked to see a dog that was having some problems. As the dog walked towards me, I had that strong tin can taste in my mouth. I knew then that the dog had vaccinosis, and I was able to tell the dog's people how to detox the dog and get it back to good health with a healthy diet and so on. Now, we know dogs have to be vaccinated for rabies by law, but energetically I find the amounts of vaccinations, mainly the preservatives, often cause them a lot of harm. It's scary how young we start injecting things into their bodies before their immune system even starts working fully. It is my belief that having a very healthy diet and lifestyle helps them build their own strength and their own immune system.

I want to share one last story. I was asked to do a reading for a horse that came from the race world. He was in a place called a sanctuary, but it really wasn't a sanctuary or safe, and he was living in horrible conditions. The people who rescued the horse contacted me to do a reading with him. This request came through an email and they had sent pictures, so I had an answer prepared for them. But when I was typing the email, this very special horse told me that he wanted there to be more healing, and he asked me to offer the three women who ran "the sanctuary" a healing for themselves. I have so much admiration for people who go in hands-on to these kinds of places, and I didn't know that I could do that myself, emotionally.

The horse showed me an image of an infant and I reached out and held it in my arms. I felt complete unconditional love for the infant, and the horse told me that this was one of the three women from the "sanctuary." He told me that each of the three women had suffered childhood abuse, which had an effect on how they operated the "sanctuary." He asked me to offer healing energy for each of the women by holding each one, one at a time, in my arms as if they were infants, and saying the words that one would need to hear to feel loved, secure and cherished in their life. The horse told me that the cycle of abuse doesn't end unless there is an offer of love to shift energy. So that's what he had me do. What is more innocent than a child in your arms that is pure, and you are offering these words of unconditional love? When you do that, there is no way for that energy not to be reached, and what powerful changes it has, we do not know, but it brings a shift, and that is what this horse taught me. I have since used this form of healing many times, and I have shared this technique along the way. If anyone were to try this approach to help someone, they first need to ask the person's or the animal's higher self for permission.

I have had the honor of doing animal communication and animal healing in places far and wide. I have read elephants in sanctuaries, horses in Germany, and dogs in New Zealand, etc. It's the vibration that travels. It doesn't matter if the animal is alive or crossed through, or where they are in the world; I can offer distance healing or assist them anywhere, often while sitting on my couch with my cats sitting on me, assisting me.

My business is called Earth Talk, and the name came to me in a meditation that I did years ago. It is about communicating with the earth, and helping to clear and shift the energy when there is an imbalance. Sometimes people ask me to come to talk to bees to see what they want in the land, and sometimes I am asked to read the land itself, and the trees, to find out what's going on. An imbalance in the land can affect the energy of the land and the people who live there. Whether I talk to people, animals, or anything in nature, it's the same concept of healing energy.

Often people call me to connect with their animal, and when they've learned what else I do, I end up reading the land as well. Sometimes this comes about because there might be a lot of illness in a household for no known reason. I once worked with a client whose daughter lived on the adjacent property, and the whole family kept getting ill. I had been there to see the horses, and they asked me to do a geopathic zone healing of the land. Geopathic healing is basically about energetic lines that go through the land which frequently need to be diverted. There are different techniques to help shift the energy, and sometimes people have had me come and point out where these are and how to shift them. I usually do this work with crystals, and some people do it with a copper stick. There are many different ways.

It is important to know that with any energy work, it is my personal belief that it's about intention. I think the more we strengthen our intentions to have higher vibrational thoughts, and I'm grateful that animals boost that up for me, it is better for our health and immune system. I always want to leave people and animals feeling empowered. I want them to know the healing will always come from them, not their healer. People and animals are their own healers in that regard, and many times with the land too. The land will show an imbalance whether it's with the people around them or some other reason.

"Intention is the key, hold it with reverence." That came from an automatic writing. I am not a person who goes to church regularly, but that was a message from Jesus. This is the way it came across when I was writing it, or more specifically, Jesus wrote it. I have received profound wisdom from Jesus through my meditations. He came through to me wearing blue jeans and

a white T-shirt and not religious at all. He showed me how I was hearing the animals with my heart, which is why I say that way of communicating goes very, very deep with me. I honestly have no words which are adequate to explain that powerful experience with Jesus completely. That's really where I'm coming from. I grew up going to a Russian Orthodox Church, my brothers and I are first generation born here, but I realize I am much more spiritual now than I ever was, and I believe God is a very benevolent God because of the animals. This is how Jesus showed me that the animals are like Him. It has to do with loving unconditionally.

For more information or to set up an appointment for a reading or healing with Kathryn, she can be reached through her email kdrage4animals@gmail.com, *or Facebook page at Earth Talk.*

Chapter 16

Reverend Andrea Goodman-Priestess of Maat, Astrologer

I was extremely honored that this extraordinary woman agreed to be a part of this book. Reverend Andrea Goodman's very unique healing gifts, techniques and vast knowledge about the languages of astrology and sound healing, are truly remarkable. Her wisdom and way of explaining life and its stages through astrology are thought provoking.

A few months after the interview, I met with Reverend Andrea in person to go over my personal birth chart, which she had prepared beforehand. The information that came forth was profound. It was a very special gift to sit in her warm and cozy house, drinking tea and hearing about the alignment of the sun, moon, and planets at the exact time of my birth, and the influences the chart has, and will continue to have, on my life. The reading validated not just my personality traits and relationships with accuracy, but also deeper insights, for example, the fact that I have always been introverted and require time to be alone with my thoughts. Reverend Andrea said that my introverted-ness was serving a purpose in my life, and is healing something from a past life. Then she explained something that my chart indicated, that

If someone asks me what my work is, I always have to list everything I do because it's not just one thing. I think of myself primarily as a singer, because that's how my career really began. I am also a voice teacher, but then teaching became less and less about vocal technique and more and more about sound healing, which is allowing sound to pour through us. Alongside that, I studied astrology and began doing readings for people. I began studying astrology in 1981, and I began reading professionally around 1985. I have been working professionally as an astrologer for thirty-five years, and the sound healing about the same amount of time.

In this most recent pandemic year, I have done more astrology than anything because that can be done over distance. I have offered some of the sound healing over the Internet as well. I should share that my teaching is not only about sound healing, but also raising spiritual consciousness, you might say. That comes through in the reading, in the healing, or in the group session. I have a weekly meditation group, and I use tarot cards as a divination for myself and also in my work with others, along with sound healing and astrology. That is a whole other aspect of what I do.

I came to astrology as a client when I lived in New York City in my 20s and 30s. When I had just been there for a year, and I believe I was about twenty-two, I went to an astrologer, Alethea Worden, for the first time at the suggestion of a friend. I continued to go every year on my birthday for about five years. After that, I felt driven to learn it, and to learn the language of it, because astrology is a language of symbols. It can be accessible to anyone, but until someone wants to learn it, it seems obscure. I had to ask my astrologer, over and over again, what is Venus? Or what is Jupiter? I just began to read voraciously about astrology. I was so obsessed, all of a sudden, which corresponded with an astrological aspect which I was experiencing at the time, which I didn't fully understand, but I just felt the impulse to study. Within a week of staying up until four in the morning reading, I had learned how to cast a chart and I sorted out the books--which ones were superficial and which ones were deeper. Then I asked my astrologer if she would teach a class. She said that she was glad to do that, and brought together a small group. As I studied with her, I also continued to see Alethea as my astrologer, and I went to her with questions. I just started to look at everyone's charts around me. I never thought that I would be reading professionally, but I was fascinated.

Each of us is unique, and the shape of that is described in the birth chart. Therefore, every chart is different. If you know the people as you're doing the charts, you can see how the pattern of symbols is expressed through the person. It is endlessly fascinating. I am always learning new things. It is not a fixed body of knowledge, because symbols are multidimensional and can be interpreted in many ways. It is infinitely creative. If you are looking at someone's Venus for example, it could be speaking about relationships, or it could be speaking about the arts, or it could be speaking about an artistic appreciation, and it will be in any of the twelve signs of the zodiac, and in any one of the twelve houses. It might be in a close relationship with a different planet, which will color it, so there is so much to say about it.

There is another aspect to how I read a chart, which I studied with Wendy Ashley, who lives in Maine and is a mythic astrologer. She developed a way of looking at the mythology that is connected to the stars and the planets, and their signs and houses. All of this is relevant to a person's unique purpose in this life, and the themes that will come up again and again for that person. So, I do Mythic astrology as well as Western astrology. There are, however, other types of astrology, which I have not studied.

I asked Reverend Andrea for more clarification between Mythic astrology and Western astrology.

Western astrology looks at the Sun, Moon and planets primarily, and their positions around the Earth. The astrological chart usually doesn't include stars and constellations, except for the signs of the zodiac. The fixed stars form a background for the planets and the Sun and Moon in motion, as they move through a sign of the zodiac. The zodiac is the series of constellations defining the circle of planetary motion around the Earth. The way that the zodiac is organized, the circle is divided up into twelve 30° divisions, and each one is assigned a constellation that is in the path of the Sun, the Moon and the planets as they move through the sky. But the twelve constellations are not at even 30° intervals in the sky. Astrology takes the convention of equal divisions around the Earth. So, it includes those twelve signs of the zodiac, but not all the other constellations in the sky, and doesn't necessarily give weight to specific stars.

The realm of Mythic astrology is to pay attention to specific stars that will be at the same degrees as the planets, and to explore the archetypes in the mythology associated with stars and constellations. Astrology is oriented to the geometry of the circle to locate bodies in space by the degrees of the zodiacal signs, and it's all from the point of view of the Earth, because that's our experience. It's not an objective astronomical view. It has the point of view that we have. We see the sun rising and setting, in other words, seemingly going around us. Even though we know we are going around it, that is not our perspective. Astrology, as I work with it, is very person centered, geocentric, that is earth centered.

I don't know if that's too much information about the way it is set up, but what it offers people is a language for speaking about who one is, that is not really psychological. Of course, there is psychology in everything human, but it's not my focus. I'll just say that my belief is that we each have a soul, and that our souls choose the moment of our birth because there is a special pattern. That's what the astrological chart reflects, the Universe at that moment, that positioning of the planets in the sky in relation to the Earth at a specific moment. That unique pattern gives our souls the very best combination of energies to fulfill what our souls come into embodiment to fulfill. I believe we come with a purpose, or several purposes, and you could call that karma. Our souls choose that moment, specifically because of the positioning of energies and patterns made by the way that the planets are arranged in the sky. We are born wide open, so we are in a sense imprinted with that pattern. I believe our souls have a wisdom, and that on that level we are choosing that pattern, because it best serves the soul's purpose--what our souls are here for.

We don't know really anything about the before and after of this life, because here we are. But I cannot accept that it is random, and I feel that there is purpose behind our coming to the planet and my belief is that this isn't all there is. I believe what it is that animates us and makes us who we are, is infinite. It is not limited to this life, and yet, to take on a physical body and to make ourselves babies, and start as infants- that has to be a huge decision on some level. I just don't think that it's random, and I believe that every soul has a journey and a mission and relationships, and significant relationships are not accidents-- they are somehow meant to be. I think that's true. It's so much bigger than we can really hold, because that means that we are all in this intricate interweaving of everybody's lives, not just each person's individual path, but each person in relation to all the others that cross our paths in one way or another. There is some big, big tapestry that includes all of us and everything that is happening, which is always shifting, changing, developing and evolving. I mean to say, it is bigger really than any of us can understand.

As a Reverend, I am ordained as a Priestess in the Ministry of Maat. Maat is the Egyptian divine being who is said to hold the order, the harmony, and the balance of the whole Universe. That is Her function. So, I think that we are always being held by Maat, and She has the big picture. I can't possibly have the big picture because I am just me, but I know that She has it. She does hold it, and there is not only the complexity of it, but a balance that is in effect.

So even when there are things in this world that we think never should have happened because they are so horrible, on some level beyond our understanding, there is a way in which it is part of a cosmic balance and a cosmic harmony that includes dissonance. Not everything is pretty, and that is part of it. There is a complexity that is beyond our understanding in terms of why. We cannot answer why to pretty much anything. We make up stories about why all the time, we try to figure it out and find who is to blame, or who gets the credit. But truly, the why is bigger than we can understand.

I love the image of being above the earth, and being aware that here are all these beings (not only human) going about their lives--and there are so many-and how can we account for everyone, take care of everyone and listen to everyone? We can't, but Maat can, or whatever divinity that we believe is holding the complete cosmos, or that there is a being who holds it, which is different than thinking that there is a being who manipulates it. I feel that there is a divine choreographer at work that has us moving in different ways, and we dance together at times. But Maat, I think of as She, is the one who is listening to everyone and balancing all the energies in some way. There is the creator divinity, who is also an aspect of what is going on, and we are certainly collaborating with that impulse. However, I think in terms of the harmony and the way that everything fits together--that is Maat.

I believe that Maat is one of the qualities of God. I don't usually use the word God myself because it has such a masculine connotation for my belief. I was raised Jewish and taught to believe that God was masculine. Throughout Christianity, and all the organized religions that we have--they are masculine-dominated. The languages speak of God as a He, and the priests, the rabbis and the gurus, for the most part are traditionally masculine. Male domination of religion disrespects half of the population. It isn't right and has created a harmful imbalance in society.

Our Ministry, so far, has only women, in order to give to women, the chance to find and claim their own spiritual authority and to have the space to allow their spiritual understanding to guide them. Not, as has been the tradition, to be spoken over by men who are used to being in authority, used to having a loud voice and used to putting themselves first. We have a different structure. It is the structure of a circle, rather than a hierarchical structure. We have a Reverend Mother, Ione, who is the one who initiated the founding of this ministry and who guides us all. Those of us who are ordained as priestesses are guides and transmitters of wisdom; we are not authority figures. Our Ministry has spread internationally wide. We have priestesses in Europe and all over North America. There are so far thirty-five or so priestesses ordained, and not all of us practice in the way that I do. We all practice differently. Some are artists and their ministry is their art, and some of us are writers, and some are healers. Mostly it is the creative and healing, intuitive artists who we are working with. That's who is attracted and who participates.

Can you explain what else you do for work as a priestess of Maat?

I perform weddings, funerals and burial services, as well as creating ceremonies for other events. I have the spiritual authority and the certification to be able to do weddings, which is a great joy in my life.

I also facilitate Cosmic Harmony groups which are about vocal sound healing. We sit together with our eyes closed and we focus on a clear intention. This could be something as simple as releasing anything that we no longer need, such as an old thought pattern. We then allow our voices to flow and release in sound. Obviously, our sounds may not be pretty if we're releasing old baggage. The sound can be whatever it needs to be to release what you've been holding onto. That's just one example. We focus on many different things in the course of a couple of hours, and you find yourself making sounds you didn't know you could make, and you find yourself feeling transformed. It really has to be experienced. It cannot be described. When I do a one-on-one healing session, I facilitate you making sound and me witnessing, or the two of us making sound together, or I can sing to you. I can give a healing and you receive it like a massage. I do not know what the sounds that I make will be; I don't know in advance. I am focused on you and trusting what comes intuitively to my imagination and what sounds come through my voice. I always ask for my Guidance and my client's Guidance to put the words and the sounds in my mouth that are most needed. So, there is another dimension of channeling. I feel almost more of a medium as a sound healer than I do as an astrologer, though when I am giving a reading, I don't know what I'm going to say before I begin. I do always ask the guides to help me, to put the words in my mouth. I am reading symbols, I am not reading text, so I don't know where the actual words that I say are coming from. What I do is different from Phyllis, a friend who is a medium, who just taps in and it comes through her for her client. I have the lens of the astrology that I feel like I'm reading, but the words that come out perhaps are channeling.

I live on Barter's Island, which is near Boothbay Harbor. I work out of my home, and I call it Ruby-Throated Spirit. I have a room that I call my studio, which is where I give readings, and I also have my piano there for voice lessons, if anyone wants that kind of vocal work. I do tarot readings and consultations there as well. I have another room that I call the meditation room, where I work with groups of people and do Reiki and sound healing work. I also have a labyrinth outside of my house in the woods that is more like a meditation walk. Mine is not a traditional labyrinth, because the shape that I had to work with is long and narrow, rather than a typical round or square labyrinth. I put a bench in the middle so that you can sit and rest there. It's an outdoor sanctuary.

I asked Rev. Andrea about daily horoscopes that you read in the newspaper and what validity she thinks they have, if any. I confessed that I still read my horoscope daily, for whatever that's worth, and that I am a Libra.

I think horoscopes are not completely made up, but I don't know what they are taking into consideration. There is something informing what they write that has to do with where the Sun is in its cycle.

The Sun is a symbol of our life force and our identity. We each have a Sun and the Sun can be in any of the twelve signs. For example, if your Sun is in Libra, then you know yourself to be a person who really wants to be in harmony in relations with other people. Relationships are very important typically for Libra, not that a Libra cannot be alone. But even if one is alone, they are always thinking of other people and how they are connected. The Libra is all about relationships, and it is an air sign. There are three airs, three earths, three waters, and three fires. The air sign is typically more mental, but of course you also have a moon, which is emotional, and Venus, which is about your heart and how you receive and give love. There are just so many other factors. If we just focus on the Sun, I think of Libra as an air sign who carries the ideals, the mental construct or knowing of love, beauty, harmony, justice, and balance. Libra wants to make peace with everybody and to get along, but Libra also knows what love should look like and holds relationships to a high standard.

I believe that general (Sun sign) astrology does have some validity, but it cannot possibly express the complexity of each person.

Astrology gives the person a way to see the complexity that you are, the strength and the gifts that you are born with, that you are always using whether you are aware of it or not, the difficulties or the challenges that might come up in your life and things that you tend to grapple with. It can describe your relationships with your parents and their relationship with each other, as parts of you, because of course we integrate or absorb our parents and carry them with us. It also speaks about which areas of life seem to be most important or that we express ourselves through.

The chart has a wheel with twelve pie pieces, and the pie pieces are called houses, and they each describe an area of life. Planets are the symbols of all our parts, you could say, and then the sign that the Sun or the Moon or the planet is in, gives the specific quality that it is expressed through. For example, Mars is the part of us that takes action, has courage, and is energetic and powerful. We all have that part of us, but with some people it's more overt, more on the outside or louder, and that depends on what sign Mars is in. If you have Mars in a fire sign, it is much more apt to be very active than if it is in a water sign. In water, Mars is more emotional and comes through you as caring for people or tuning into people emotionally. Water signs have more to do with emotions. Mars in an earth sign, will express as hard-working and practical, and be apt to put the energy into physical things.

So, each planet is a part of us, and each planet can be in any of the twelve signs, depending on when you were born, which gives its quality. And the house that it is in, is the part of your life that is highlighted. So, it is different to have the Sun, which is how you express your own identity, in the house of home, for example, then it is to have it in the house of career. If the sun is in the fourth house, the person knows herself in her home or nest, and the person who has the Sun in the 10th house knows herself when she is visible, effective, and out in the world doing things that can gain recognition of some kind. Both are the Sun, and either could be Libra for instance, but where in life it is best expressed, is described by the houses.

The relationship between the planets is also important. For example, if the Sun is in Libra, and the Sun is in conjunction together with Venus, which is the ruler of Libra, then it's like a double Libra, and it is very concerned about relationships and beauty. Those two themes, that we think of as feminine, become more important. Also, I would say that a person who has a Sun-Venus conjunction and is a woman, has chosen very specifically to be a woman this time around, if you believe in reincarnation. Although I certainly know men who have Sun-Venus conjunctions and they tend to be more sensitive than many other men.

Each chart is so unique and complex, and when someone comes for a reading, I can show them what their soul has chosen for them. They will bring their life experience to what they are hearing, and they can tell me or not tell me--and I love it when they do tell me--how it resonates for them, how they see that they have lived that out, and what it looks like in their lives. So, it's a way to understand oneself and to accept oneself. I think that's a big gift of astrology. When you see how unique you are, the ways that you may have thought you were strange, different, inadequate, or didn't fit in, or were not like everyone else around you, can be reframed completely. You might now say, "I wasn't supposed to be able to do that, and that is not at all where my passion lies, or what I am good at, or what I came here for. So, to compare myself with someone who is good at that is totally meaningless."

Our culture is so based on comparison, hierarchy, winners and losers, I don't know who gets away without some kind of wound to their self-esteem. Our culture is based on winning and losing, and judgment. In light of your uniqueness, that kind of judgment is irrelevant and meaningless, and astrology shows you that. It says, yes, you are you, and you are meant to be you, and here are the things that make you, you, and to celebrate them.

There's a whole other piece of it which is that the planets and the Sun and Moon of course, keep moving all the time. There was a moment when you were born--that was a special moment––and then everything kept moving. As they move, they reflect your evolution, and how you grow. So that way I can see what themes are up for you now, by which planets are moving through which houses. Saturn, particularly, is the planet of the structure of things. When it moves through a house, and it will spend two and a half years or so in that house, it will re-structure that area of life. You might move if Saturn is moving into your fourth house, but not necessarily; you might be just taking care of things that needed attention and making your foundations firmer. There are different ways to interpret those movements and there are specific times for a shift in focus in your life. I can see that when I look at where the planets are moving now, in relation to your birth chart.

That is the gift of understanding that everything is always in motion. So, when we feel stuck, it is not the truth of it. We are not really stuck unless we are judging ourselves for not doing something that we are not doing. But if we can be with the stillness, or the silence, then we can understand that something is moving at an inner level at that time, and needs the time and space, either to integrate what has happened or to gestate what is about to be born in us. And so, it lifts an awful lot of self-judgment and helps us understand that we are right where we are supposed to be, that things are moving and will be resolved and will shift into a new energy when it is the right time.

Wow. At this point I said to Rev. Andrea that her words were so profound and comforting to me.

I think that is what I am here for, to help people to be happy with their lives and with who they are and how things are evolving.

I asked Rev. Andrea to explain the meaning of a Saturn Return- something which I have heard about from other mediums in previous readings. Because I was fifty-nine years old at the time of this interview, I believed that I was perhaps in a Saturn Return time of my life.

Each planet has its own rate of motion and its own timing of the cycles. The moon, for instance, goes all the way around the Earth every month. That's what a month is. The sun makes its way around the zodiac in a year. Each planet has its own timing, and the Saturn cycle is twenty-nine years. You have just completed your second Saturn cycle, and your Saturn is at 23° Capricorn, so your Saturn Return was a year ago in January. You have completed it and now you are in the beginning of a new cycle, so that's what you're feeling, and it is kind of like, now what? And how do I begin?

The thing is that when we are born, we are born into a certain structure which is given to us by our family, our religion and the culture surrounding us. So that's the Saturn structure that you are born with, and that will provide a foundation for you always. When you have lived a whole twenty-nine years in that structure and you've learned it, rebelled against it, and tried to find your place within it, when you get to twenty-nine, you can let go of that structure and create a new one that is based more on your own inner necessity--what you know of yourself, rather than what your parents expected of you.

The second cycle that you just completed is really about making your mark on the world, such as having a family, if you do, or having a career, if you do, and developing your interests, skills, and accomplishing things in the world. When that cycle is complete, there's a different kind of relationship to the world and to your place in it. The third cycle is more about two things. I'll say one is to honor what really, really delights you and what you really, truly want for yourself, what fulfills your deep desires for yourself, your creative desire, and your passions, because that last cycle was so much about serving others around you. And it's also about leaving a legacy of some kind, or imparting what you've learned, and sharing what you know or what you've gathered. It's very personal and at the same time it's more universal. It is both. I think there's a great freedom in that period.

I am sixty-seven, so I am already well into this third Saturn cycle. I think of it as the wisdom cycle, where you've gathered a lot of experience and knowledge, and you're not trying to prove anything anymore. There is not that anxiety around being worthy and being worth existing. It's like, I've existed for sixty years and I'm here, and I don't have to prove that I deserve to be here. It gets easier on that level, and it's not like you can't be hurt by rejection or whatever, but it's not the same 'all or nothing' feeling around everything. It's just a different time of life. If you think about our archetype of the grandparents, though not all grandparents are the same, there is an archetype that we carry within us of a grandparent, and that is someone who is patient, kind and loving and sort of has a sparkle in her eye--kind of delight in every little thing. Those qualities, I definitely feel have been growing in me in my sixties. What you're doing in this period will leave a legacy; this book, for instance, and other projects that you may want to fulfill, and you are sharing what you uniquely have come to understand through your life experience. Not everyone has to make a book, but for you, you are making a book and highlighting what fascinates you and what gives you joy, delight and wonder.

By the time your third cycle ends, you might be eighty-seven and I don't know that anyone gets another twenty-nine years, but if we could, we go into a fourth cycle. I think of these three cycles as corresponding to the triple goddess: we begin with the maiden in the first Saturn cycle, then the mother in the second, and in the third cycle, the crone form of the feminine. The maiden is that first cycle of being open and innocent. The mother is the time of the giving and taking care of everyone. The crone is the wisdom phase, the elder, the wise one. Women who are no longer worried about men's appreciation of them are very powerful. Men are afraid of them, and they often feel compelled to put them down. Our generation is changing the values that we've been raised with. In this culture only young women were valued, but we are changing that today.

I asked Rev. Andrea to explain what it means when Mercury is in retrograde.

Mercury Retrograde has to do with the fact that the planets are not really going around the Earth, as it appears; we are all going around the sun at different rates. However, astrology is looking at the sky from the Earth, so as we look at the sky, we see a planet and it will seem to be going in one direction through the signs, and it will seem to stop and go backwards for a while. Mercury is the fastest because it's the closest to the sun, so it will do that more often than the other planets, usually three or four times a year. So, it appears to go backwards, over the same degrees that it just went through, and it will go forward again, so it will go over those same degrees three times. That sets up a process with Mercury around your thinking, your mind and your communication.

They say that when Mercury is retrograde, communications can be easily misunderstood or certain logical things, like mechanical things, will go haywire. Timing, for instance, like scheduling appointments, might have to be changed because people forget about their appointments, or things will fall between the cracks. The logic behind that is that Mercury is the symbol for the mind, which usually functions in a very linear chain of thought that goes in a forward direction, but when Mercury is in retrograde, we are held back to go over where we've been. Sometimes I find myself in a Mercury retrograde phase looking at old pictures, or old things I've written which I haven't looked at in a long time, or going back over something that happened and am pulled off mentally into kind of a daydream around something. Our minds are easily distracted by past things and it's a very good time for picking up any loose ends that we have overlooked around a project. For example, if you're on a project and you're busy with it, sometimes you can't take care of every detail and you say, I'll do that later. When Mercury is retrograde, that is a good time to go back over those details and put them in their place, weave them into the fabric, and to go back over certain memories that kind of stick with you, that you want to understand better, with a new perspective. So, Mercury retrograde is good for those things, but when everybody is off in a daydream, it's easy to forget appointments or to overlook certain things, like to miss an email. That kind of thing happens a lot in a Mercury retrograde because of this distractedness that is happening.

That's the interpretation of Mercury retrograde, and the other planets can also go retrograde, and they do, except the sun and moon, because we really are going around the sun, and the moon really is going around us. It's the phenomenon like when you're in a car and you see someone up ahead on a bicycle, and as you pass them, they appear to go backwards as you go forward for a while, and then when you go around the curve you see that they are going forward. It's that illusion; that's the phenomenon. When other planets are in retrograde, typically whatever the theme of that planet is becomes more internal or more interior for you. Jupiter is the planet of expansion, enthusiasm and growth. Things may seem to be growing and expanding but usually, in retrograde, it's under the surface.

I asked Rev. Andrea for an explanation about the Age of Aquarius, something of which I have become very fascinated with since conducting interviews for this book.

The Ages are the time blocks that are approximately 2000-2400 years, though I've heard different lengths. What that is about has to do with what they call precession as opposed to procession, meaning the backwards movement of the Equinoxes. March 21 is the equinox moment when day and night are equal, and we always start the astrological year there, which is the beginning of Aries. That's how the astrological year is understood to be. But in fact, that was true 4,000 years ago, so about 2000 BCE is when the age of Aries began, and that was a time of the Greeks and the Hebrews and honoring the Ram (Aries symbol). In Judaism there is something called a shofar which is a Ram's Horn, and it is blown to herald a new year. About 2,000 years after the beginning of that time, we moved into the Age of Pisces. It means that the Spring Equinox actually has been occurring against the backdrop of Pisces. I don't know who made the decision to start time over again (counting time to our current year), that's the common era that we think of, but these last 2,000 years have been the age of Pisces. In this period, the predominant mythology has been all about Jesus, not about the sky, whereas before that, there was this relationship to the sky and the constellations in the sky, and all of the mythology was about the sky. There was a shift from the Age of Taurus which was the time of more of a matriarchal society to the Age of Aries and a patriarchal society, beginning with the Hebrews, the Sumerians and the Greeks. Then Christianity took over and that's been the era that we've been in.

Now we are shifting from that Age of Pisces into the Age of Aquarius, which is the next sign going backwards through the zodiac. The exact beginning of that is not a certain date, but a gradual evolution, and the Age of Aquarius then, is beginning, or has begun--people see it differently. It's much more about the valuing of each individual, as well as the consciousness of the collective. So, understanding that we are all in this together, is an Aquarian point of view. It's about wanting a democracy, which is an Aquarian ideal, for instance, where everyone gets one vote, and each vote is counted, not just those of an elite ruling class. That whole concept is Aquarian.

Aquarius is very much about finding a new way, so all the new technology is very Aquarian and that has been exponentially growing already, and that will continue. If we think of a god or a goddess in every culture, in the Age of Taurus it was the Goddess, and in the Age of Aries, it shifted over to a masculine God and then it shifted over to this divine human (Jesus). Now it has shifted over into each one of us. I would say it is taking responsibility for our own divinity and our own understanding of what is divine. You cannot tell someone else what God is. It really has to be in each of our hearts, and it's not something that you can impose. It is something each of us needs to discover. I think the Aquarian Age is really when we are each going to be aware of our own inner guru and we need to respect everybody else's in the same way that we value our own. I think that is what the Aquarian ideal is about.

However, the Aquarian age has just begun, or is just beginning. I think we had a big boost into it this year because the two planets Saturn and Jupiter, together, moved into Aquarius at the same time, on the Winter Solstice (in 2020), and they were exactly together at the 0 degree of Aquarius. Saturn is the commitment, and Jupiter is the expansion, so we are committing to the expansion of finding a new way so that it works for everybody. This is what I believe the times are about, not that it is necessarily a great or easy time, and there is always a resistance and fear of change and plenty of complexity, but that is what wants to happen.

I am very optimistic for us, because we are finding new ways. I also feel the (Covid) pandemic has been an alchemical transformative time that forced us to be still, to just stop what we have been doing; stop the momentum. We're being asked to find new ways for what needs to be done, for what is screaming to be done, using new technology, and being very creative and inventive. Coming out of that, we are not the same as we were, and we really don't know what's ahead, but it will grow out of who we have become through this transformation. It's hard for us to wrap our heads around, because we won't be alive through the next 2000 years. We will only be doing our part in our own time.

     Maine Mediums, Mystics and Healers

We were raised in the age of Pisces, so we are bringing our learned biases to it, and at the same time we are evolving, growing and changing. Everybody is, no matter what it looks like. Everyone is in the process of doing our part and it is not for us to say that no one should do this or that part. People are doing the part they are doing, and we don't know why, but I think that the extremism we see is really provoking a commitment to the values that really, really matter to us. It is making everybody say no, that is not who we are--that is not what we want.

Can you explain more about who you are as a writer?

I write for myself, but I have published a book called *Lightning Holds my Hand, A Woman's Journal of Guidance,* that is taken from my journals during the period of my divorce in 2002 and into the beginning of 2003. It was a period of my life when I was desperate and asked for help. I had been reading other channeled literature, and I didn't know that I would be able to get answers, but I just asked because I had nowhere else to turn. I wrote what came to me from my Guidance, and I call it my Guidance because it didn't have any other name. It's not like I channeled an Archangel or other entity. When I asked, "Who are you?" the answer was,

"I am the one who knows you, who has loved you, witnessed you, cried with and comforted you, who walks with you, sings with you. I am you and you are I."

Every time I asked that question, I got that answer, so I simply call it my Guidance. Maybe it's a part of me, but it's not a part of me that I am in touch with most of the time, unless I ask. The Guidance was always compassionate and always comforting and always reframed what was happening in such a way that I could be peaceful, though it was not a peaceful time. It was a very, very disruptive time in my life, and I was very frightened for my future. My daughter was ten and I didn't know how we were going to manage everything. I kept asking for help and I kept getting such wise words. I would be amazed because it would completely turn me around. I would read it to my friends and say, listen to this, listen to what came when I asked. People would ask, can I have a copy of that? Over and over again, people would want the words for themselves. So, I decided to make it a book, and then we published it through the Ministry. So, it exists. It is a book, and people can read it. It helps people. It's not just about divorce, it's about any traumatic change. That Guidance is there and still, if ever I ask about anything, I get an answer.

That is a level of mediumship, I guess, and eventually I found that I was able to communicate with my father, for example, or others who had passed, but it came for me through the writing as a state of listening that I was able to go into. If I asked a question, it was like opening the channel and then I heard what came to me and I trusted it. That is another aspect of my work, and I also write poetry and the poetry doesn't usually feel like channeling, but it still makes itself known on some level. When I sit down to write, something comes through my hand that I didn't know was coming. That's another aspect of what I do.

A few times people have asked me, "Does your Guidance have words for me?" So, I have asked, and I have gotten words for people that were helpful for whatever they were going through, sometimes in surprising ways. That's another dimension of it, but it all feels related to me, and that is why I was so happy to be able to call myself a Priestess once I was ordained, because then suddenly everything that I do, even keeping the fire going and cooking, is all part of priestess work, and then everything made sense. I didn't have to say, well I am really a singer, but I do astrology, or I am an astrologer, but this is what you need to know. It's always been a little confusing to define myself, but if I am simply a priestess that includes all of it in my mind, although few people know what that means.

How did you learn to develop your sound healing practice?

I lived in New York City in my 20s and 30s and I had not really chosen to be a performer, but I met an amazing singer and composer and theater director, named Meredith Monk. She and I just hit it off and she asked me to sing with her. I began studying voice, and taking dance classes, although I had never thought of myself as being a performer. In order to do my best, I needed to train, so I did that. Her music was without words, and so I began to use my voice as an instrument, for sound itself, and to let the voice do all the things that it can do, and to create music. We did a lot of collaborative work, creating and using the different sounds our voices could make. It was not conventional work at all. I was very young, so I just took to it, and I thought it was beautiful. I participated with her, and I did my best and that became a very full career. I made five record albums with her, and a couple of films, and we toured all over Europe and the US and Canada, and places like Israel, Japan, and Yugoslavia. It was a big performing career.

My way of singing included singing in highs and lows and I could use every vocal quality that I felt was needed for what we were doing. That gave me a vocabulary of sound that not many people have, because most people sing with words and the voice is there to carry the words. Of course, people have their own unique sound, but the focus usually isn't so much on the nuances of sound. It is on the transmission of the song. That was a very different vocal preparation. I also took voice lessons with a great voice teacher, John Devers, and I was already performing when I came to him. He gave me the technique I needed to do what Meredith was asking of me. He taught me how to use my voice in a very big and healthy way with a lot of resonance, and I think you can hear it even with my speaking voice. It's a resonance that I have learned to make. He taught me to use every part of my voice and to go back and forth between lower and upper registers. So, I have that vocal technique as well. I always say that my teacher John Devers gave me my vocal instrument, and Meredith gave me my vocabulary.

Later I took a brief weekend workshop with a woman who taught voice as a healing instrument and that piece of it is intuitive. You ask the person what they need, and you hold that in your mind, and you find sound in your mind, and you try to make that sound, and you stay with it and let it grow and develop. That practice felt totally natural for me, and I found that I could see inside the person. For instance, the person didn't say he had tension in the back of his neck, but I felt it. So, with my sound, I worked to ease that tension and afterward he reported that he felt ease of tension in the back of his neck, without previously telling me that he had tension there. So that confirmed for me that I was seeing accurately and that my sound was affecting a change. That was the beginning of the sound healing work.

Then, as with the astrology, I just started trying it on everybody. At a certain point, Ione, the Rev. Mother of our

Ministry--though this was before the Ministry was established--she was teaching journal workshops and dream workshops. I was studying with her, and she invited me to teach sound healing in tandem with a workshop about dreams. We took a group of women for a weekend retreat, and I began teaching the sound healing work. Then I began teaching in other places and found that anyone could learn it. The more you know your voice, the more vocabulary you have to work with, but anyone can heal with sound.

When I moved to Maine, I married a doctor, and I had a child. However, I didn't have a context for my healing work here at first. I offered a voice and movement class, and I had a few students who began to come. Initially, I was teaching them vocal technique and physical movement work that involved releasing and strengthening, and gradually they wanted the intuitive sound healing work. At a certain point I came to call it "Cosmic Harmony."

I have been in Maine for over thirty years now, as I moved here in 1989. I began teaching that class thirty-one years ago. Over the years I have developed the sound healing work in groups, as well as doing it individually with people. I know I have so much in me for vocabulary and possibility for sound, and for that reason, I can be very specifically responsive to the person I am singing to or with. It also incorporates all the work that I did with Meredith Monk, and I owe her so much gratitude for bringing me along in her work and imparting so much to me.

I want to express gratitude for all my teachers, mentors, students, colleagues and friends. All of them have contributed beyond measure to my professional and spiritual journey, which I have described as a path like water--having no defined shape but inevitably finding its way down the mountain, joining other streams, eventually merging with the great ocean.

Andrea can be contacted through her website, www.rubythroatedspirit.com

Chapter 17

Alice Bizier King-Spiritual Table Tipping Physical Mediumship

Alice King is a gifted medium clairvoyant who incorporates a blend of healing modalities through the physical mediumship of table tipping sessions with her clients. I enjoyed a healing reading with her which gave me closure about a close friend who passed away a few years ago. It was very unexpected and comforting to hear from this person, and Alice's upbeat attitude and accuracy made it a moving experience for me.

Alice was very interesting to talk to and the following is a summary of our enlightening conversation.

It fascinates me that Modern Spiritualism basically started with a form of table tipping. In 1848, the young Fox sisters of Hydesville, New York began hearing unexplained rapping sounds on the furniture and in the walls of their bedroom, and other strange things began to happen. The sisters, Maggie and Kate (age fourteen and eleven,) started rapping in response to what they had heard, and found themselves communicating with a spirit. Their mother started asking questions and the spirit would answer simple questions correctly with a pattern of rappings.

By developing a communication code with the spirit, the sisters learned that it was Charles B. Rosna, a peddler who had been murdered in the house five years earlier and buried in the cellar. Communication with Charles B. Rosna's spirit was the beginning of Modern Spiritualism.

I am a psychic medium. Psychics read people's energy. A medium sees and gets messages from loved ones in spirit. Spiritual Table Tipping is a form of physical mediumship because we are using an object, a table, for Spirit to communicate through. At a table tipping session, the energy of our loved ones or spirit guides comes through the table and they answer our questions by tipping or tilting the table, once for "no" and twice for "yes." The top of the three-legged table I have, also spins on the pedestal to communicate to us that a spirit is leaving and another loved one is coming through. You can actually feel the essence and excitement of your loved ones come through the table. Loved ones will also hug you by leaning on your lap. You can really feel the energy of unconditional love coming through, which is very healing. How amazing and healing it is to feel the essence and to hear from your loved ones that they are at peace and that they love you, which is something that they might not have been capable of doing or telling you during their life here on earth.

Communication, either with loved ones who have passed on, or with one's spirit guides, such as guardian angels, can assist a person with questions about health, relationships, career, or just whether they're on the right path in life. We can find out if you have blocks physically or spiritually. We can check on your soul plan and what that is, to find out where people are stuck in life. People can bring their own questions to ask Spirit. Sometimes people get discombobulated and once they get to the table tipping session, they forget to ask their written question. In this case, Spirit has a different agenda. Spirit guides will come through and let me as a medium know what the person needs to know, and prompt me to ask the questions that are helpful. It is Spirit who is giving them the answer by the movement of the table, not me. I am merely being used as a conduit to bring information and healing to the people at the table.

I don't believe in evil as an entity. I believe the only thing that is evil is the dense energy of emotions such as anger, pain, shame, guilt, or unhealthy grief. For example, unresolved grief can be very dense energy because it's not necessarily healthy. These negative energies come through the table. They come through to help us become aware that we are carrying them and Spirit is available to help us release them. Many times, releasing these energies helps us "feel lighter" and heal physical pain. Someone who has chronic shoulder discomfort might feel this discomfort lesson or alleviated altogether. During table tipping, it is Spirit doing the healing.

Clients get validation from their loved ones that they are legitimately coming through the table. Clients can feel the essence of their energy or give us messages to validate. At one session, I was doing table tipping with a woman named Joan. Her close friend Claire was coming through the table. I saw Claire holding a toaster of some sort, so I asked Joan, "Why is she showing me a toaster?" Joan chuckled and replied,

"When Claire was here on earth, I would say, 'I love you.'" Claire would always respond,

"I love you more than my toaster!" Joan could not believe it!

At another recent table tipping session there was a woman, Judy, whose mother was unable to raise her, so she lived with her grandparents. Her mother came through in the session. I told her that her mother was showing me a fish bowl with water in it and just one fish. I asked her if she understood why her mother would be showing me a fish bowl. I asked her all these questions and then I finally told her I literally saw her with the fish bowl under her arm, and that she was running with it, and water was sloshing all over the place, but the one fish was still intact and safe. The woman explained the grandparents who raised her were abusive, and she always wondered who would think to give a child to these people. She said, "I always said that my grandparents should never have been allowed to raise even a fish in a fishbowl!" Judy's healing message that day was that her mom, who was carrying her in the fish bowl, loves her dearly and is always with her and protecting her.

During spiritual table tipping, healing is also being accomplished through other techniques such as Reiki or shamanic practices. This can include a power animal retrieval, soul retrieval, ancestral healing, removal of dense energies, cord cutting, past life healing and psychopomping- helping an earthbound spirit cross to the other side. It's very intriguing. I once had the future father of a young girl come through during a table tipping session. He came in to tell her that she needed to connect with her emotions to be ready for her next lifetime. He was so adamant. I could not emphasize enough how important that was to her father from the future. Connecting with emotions is important so you can set healthy boundaries. I had never encountered that before. Whatever Spirit gives me, I have to say it, whether I understand it or not, because Spirit will keep repeating the message if I don't pass the message along. There's no such thing as time and space on the other side, because everything is happening at the same time. The father from the girl's future came through to give her the message for healing.

Soul retrieval is sometimes needed when a person goes through a traumatizing event and a part of that person's soul separates from them. It is a survival mechanism at the time. However, what helped us as a child to survive does not necessarily help us as an adult. An example of soul retrieval is when this young man, named Brad, was fourteen years old and experienced the trauma of unexpectedly losing his grandfather, whom he was very close to. In the session, his grandfather validated that it was him. I saw the grandfather handing his grandson a bowling ball. The grandson knew it was him because his grandfather had left him his bowling ball. The grandfather wanted his grandson to take up bowling again, because bowling with his grandad had always brought him great joy. The grandfather knew that Brad was not his usual joyful self since his passing. At the time of his grandfather's passing, Brad was in great pain. He felt that he should not feel joy again. It was just not right with his grandfather not being there anymore. So, he pushed joy away. The fourteen-year-old essence of living joyfully, separated from his own being. He did not realize this occurred at that time. The fourteen-year-old Brad was just protecting himself from the intense pain he felt. During the session, the client connects again with his fourteen-year-old essence of joy and experiences an increased level of joy, which was evident by his body language and a huge smile on his face.

I started doing table tipping after my brother John passed away in 2002. There were so many unusual things happening that I did not understand, and I was driving to work in tears some days. These spirit happenings frightened me. I had never experienced anything like the spirit world. One of the things that happened was that my brother's spirit image appeared in a photo that was taken with me in it. You can clearly see the outline of his full figure standing behind me and you can see an outline of an angel behind him.

When I was showing the photo to my friend Gayle at work, she stated, "John has a message for you. You need to do table tipping to find out what he wants to tell you." It frightened me, but I felt I had to do the table tipping because these happenings would continue. One evening a couple of my sisters and John's widow and a few friends did table tipping. It was an awesome and powerful experience. John came through immediately and validated it was him. I have been offering Spiritual Table Tipping ever since! It has been twenty years!

I told Alice that I always feel sorry for people who don't believe in spiritual mediumship and the benefit of getting a good reading, because they're missing out on so much peace that they could find from the experience.

There is a huge shift in energy presently in the world right now, and with this energy shift people are moving from materialism to spirituality and a higher level of consciousness. People have their own way of connecting with love, and I just choose to do spiritual work in this way. Everybody is trying to uncover that light within themselves, to increase their vibration, to become conscious of our Oneness with the God consciousness, to understand that God is Love and We are God and We are Love. I do table tipping to help people to realize this, to help them become aware of and release dense energy and replace it with love.

I consider myself a Spirit Communicator and Soul Healer. With a background of thirty-five years in nursing, my soul's mission is to serve, facilitate and inspire soul healing and create awareness and connection to the Divinity within each of us. My main goal is to prove continuity of life and to assist you with your soul evolution when you become "stuck" in your spiritual journey.

Besides being a Psychic Medium, studying at the Augusta Spiritualist Church and Morris Pratt Institute, I am a Reiki

Master and Shamanic Practitioner. I have studied Shamanism under Dory Cote at The Center of Earth Light Healing in Maine, and studied Shamanic Energy Medicine with Alberto Villoldo, Four Winds Society in Chile.

For more information and to contact Alice for a Spiritual Table Tipping email her at aliceking@seeds-of-grace.com or call 207-314-1499.

You can visit her website at www.seeds-of-grace.com. Alice offers individual or group sessions including In-Home Parties or virtual sessions via Zoom!

Chapter 18

Darlene Chadbourne- Master Numerologist
Dowser & Mentor

I am fascinated with numerology and began noticing numbers when I started seeing 11s everywhere, all the time, about eleven years ago. It seemed every time I looked at the clock it was eleven minutes past the hour. I woke up all the time at 3:11am or 5:11am. The year that I started noticing 11s, both my son and daughter were assigned the number 11 on their baseball and softball uniforms. It stunned me and it really got my attention, and still does. I mentioned it to a friend who is a medium, and she told me that 11 is a special master number and that it is associated with Spirit, and that it is also an angel validation number. I was going through a hard time in my life and that comforted me. Then, I started seeing 22s (considered another master number) and also 31, which was my mother's year of birth. As a town clerk, I see patterns in numbers on accounts and especially on license plates, and I'm pretty sure I drive people crazy pointing out "good" numbers all the time!

I was excited to talk with Darlene Chadbourne and expected some insights on my numerology reading, but I was blown away with the deeply profound information that came forth. My reading made me feel unique and special. Darlene is far more than a numerologist, she is a strong Intuitive with many gifts, who delves in many interesting spiritual activities. I could have talked with her all day long.

The following was transcribed from our conversation that day:

When people start seeing numbers, it just means that Spirit is trying to get their attention to open up their "knowing" more. I hear from so many people who say that is why they are coming to me, because they are seeing numbers and repeated numbers. It's time for you to broaden yourself and get a deeper meaning of who you are. It's no accident that you contacted me.

Freedom Through Numbers by Finding Your "I Am," is a book I have written, and the diagram in the book is what got me to this place. I am more than numerology. That diagram is from sacred geometry, and it also involves numbers.

I do numerology as a way to help me understand what your soul has set up for you when you came into this life. By reading those numbers, I can tell what your job is about, what you need to learn, and where you need to go. Then there is a timing, just like in astrology, and we have transits where we move from 1 to 9 in time periods on numerology. I also work on the time components of numerology once I do the reading for you, and I can identify when the windows of opportunity are, and when it's best to just sit back, wait, and do nothing, so that you are not wasting your time. When we get into the blueprint, I can show you how I do that. It's a guidance tool for me. My background was in psychology, and when you do psychology, you have to work on yourself before you work on anybody else. I didn't want to be in that institutional system, so I chose to work with people through numerology.

It's been a wonderful path for me and it's a jumping off place for me to work deeper with others. I have many mentoring clients that I work with, many self-employed people and entrepreneurs who want to get to where they are going.

I specialize in emotional release work that gets roadblocks out of your way. These are old beliefs that we carry, that get in the way of moving forward in our lives, caused by fears and other emotions. We release that and introduce you to new positive beliefs that allow you to move forward. That's the bigger picture of who I am, but numerology gives me the basis of why you are here in this lifetime, and what is your soul's next lesson. I believe the soul develops just like we do, and we learn things along our path, but the soul has many, many lifetimes to continue evolving. That's my overall belief.

I came to this path late in life. When I turned fifty, I decided I wanted to go to college because I had never been. At the time, I was helping my husband with his three businesses. I was running one of them, managing the bookkeeping for the other two, and I had four children and a household to run. I was pretty busy, and there was not much time for me. Something hit me when I turned fifty, so I went to college to figure out who I was.

At about this same time, I went to a psychic for a reading. After the reading she reached up on her bookshelf and she said, "They are telling me that you need to borrow this book." The book was *Numerology, and the Divine Triangle*, written by Dusty Bunker. I had that before I went to school, but I never got into it until I started studying math in college.

When I started my college geometry class, two very synchronistic events happened. One was with a client that I had on the side, as I was doing herbal consultation at the time, who took me to the Boston Museum of Science for a Leonardo da Vinci traveling display. I was very drawn to da Vinci in school, his artwork and his research. The other, was two weeks after I got back from Boston. I had an invitation in the mail to come learn how to dowse a labyrinth.

Can you explain how you went from learning to dowse, to learning numerology?

Dowsing is another skill of mine, and dowsing is commonly known by farmers using a "Y" branch to find water, but there are many uses for dowsing. The professor I had for that study, on his time off from work, would take trips to sacred sites in Europe, so he was very much into spirituality. He recommended a book for me about sacred geometry. It was on architecture and also about the study of sacred architecture of cathedrals and other special buildings. In that book, there was also a chapter on how it all came from the original nine numbers.

Spirit was at work, because I already had the numerology book, and when I saw it contained the Pythagorean transfer chart from sacred geometry, I thought, *I am going to see what this book is about.* It was all very synchronistic.

I learned more about dowsing, and then through that study, I learned numerology. So, that's how I got started on this path very late in life. I am now seventy-eight, and I have been doing this for a while.

I asked Darlene to explain more about how dowsing energy works.

Dowsing is important because we all have energy fields. I use dowsing to help people release emotional blocks. I dowse their physical, emotional, mental, and spiritual energy fields. I ask, where is their belief stuck, or what chakra is it stuck in? How can I help you replace that belief with a positive one, so you can move on with your life? Also, I don't always use L rods, I also dowse with my fingers. Dowsing trains your mind to plug into your "knowing." I can dowse people over zoom, or over the phone. I ask their higher self and spirit guides to work with my higher self and spirit guides to help get the best results for what they need at that moment in time. Then, I dowse and get answers. It has been a work in progress, and I haven't always done that work, but it's been added in the last five years or so. It is an interesting path. We all have those interesting paths, but we just need to get out of the way and let it happen.

Dowsing, whether you use L rods or your fingers or a pendulum, enables you to have a physical sign of what your intuition is telling you. If you are not at the level where it's totally intuition, you may need some outside visible signs because you are not at the place of just trusting that knowing. I am much better at that now than I used to be. Dowsing is a great place to start.

The only place that I use dowsing rods now is when I dowse the earth and the labyrinth, because it gives you the exact place where you need to be. When I use my fingers, it's harder to get the exact location.

Can you explain more about how you dowse for a labyrinth, and how you learned to dowse and build them for people? What are grids and how does that affect the creation of labyrinths?

     Maine Mediums, Mystics and Healers

All the sacred sites are built on grid conjunctions and there are many books about that, but the labyrinth that I create is very different than one which you just lay down. The reason I dowse a labyrinth as compared to just laying out a pattern, is because when you dowse it you are asking the earth, if it wants a labyrinth there, how big is it going to be and where the entrance should be to best tap into the energy of the earth?

I have some incredible labyrinth stories. There's a double one that my partner and I built six years ago in New Hampshire. One labyrinth is male and the other female, and each of them is fifty feet in diameter. If you pick those up and put them together, they're an exact mirroring of each other, and they were never measured, they were only dowsed. I dowse by using L rods. By dowsing them they're exactly fifty feet in diameter and every path is very similar.

Can you elaborate a little more on what a labyrinth is?

Labyrinths are wonderful tools, and I have installed many of them for many different people. It's about bringing heaven and earth together. That's the other part of the diagram in my book; there are five circles; the top blue one represents heaven, the bottom green one represents earth, you are in the middle circle, and the yellow circles are to the left and the right. The kundalini line goes from the center of heaven to the center of earth. When you finish a labyrinth and you get to the middle, there is a vortex that's coming down from heaven, and a vortex in the earth. That vortex of energy from above and below, comes into the heart. When you accumulate all of that energy in the heart from heaven and the earth, you give and you receive to others on the human plane. This is how you do your work. You can't just be giving, giving, giving, you also have to be receiving. Consequently, just doodling figure eights is a beautiful active meditation, and specifically just doodling the sideways figure eight, which is the infinity sign.

I was struck by this information and I told Darlene that all my life I have loved doodling daisy flowers, which are very similar to the motion of making figure eights. For me they are like doodling figure eights in a circle. I always knew that it oddly made me feel good while I was doing it. Suddenly I understood exactly what she meant by it being a form of active meditation, one of many insights I gained by talking with Darlene that day.

I know exactly what you mean. It is like that ebb and flow. There is a pattern that you might want to look at on the internet. It is the Flower of Life pattern, a symbol of circles going together, which is a sacred geometric symbol.

I asked Darlene if she thought the early people knew about the connection between sacred geometry, architecture, and sacred numbers.

I think earlier people had more of a connection to nature: the land and the heavens. They didn't have all the distractions that we have now in the modern world. We are more disconnected from nature than we ever have been, and I think that's a big piece of what is going on now in the world. Also, a big part of astronomy and astrology is that we are leaving the Piscean age and going into the Aquarian Age, which is a huge transition. 2161 years or so is about the amount of time for each astrological age. Without going into it too deeply, there are twelve signs in astrology. Aquarius is at the top, so we have now completed a whole cycle of all twelve signs. The last time we were in Aquarius was back in the Osiris Egyptian times, and this is the second time that humanity has been around to Aquarius again. Therefore, it is huge, and what they call a Great Year in astrology. I study and dabble in many things, and it all comes together.

I told Darlene that I can't get enough of learning about the Age of Aquarius, and the idea of us being upgraded as humans, as we are entering a time of attaining a higher consciousness.

We don't get to see the big picture, but this kind of knowledge allows us to think about how big the cycle is. The Egyptian times were called the Golden Age, so this is a new beginning for humanity to move to a higher consciousness and a higher level of being. This year (2022) will still be a little tumultuous, but by 2024 we really should be seeing a big difference in humanity. The Age of Aquarius song was a premonition of this time that we are in right now, and what they were talking about is what is happening right now. That song and Aquarius was open for a small window of time during the 60s, and the planets were lined up in a similar way to what they are now, and that's why we had that little window of opening.

There is a lot to it, so don't let it overwhelm you. I tell people to try to stay above the duality; be like a fly on the wall and observe. Don't get caught up in the fear. Put a bubble up around you, and let everything bounce off, with love. It can deplete your energy and that's why we need to keep that kundalini line open. Try my "I Am" exercise from my book. It can change your life.

I mentioned again to Darlene how much the astrology intrigues me and personally helps me to not get so wrapped up in the negative energy from the world events that are going on right now.

My whole life started to change when I started doing that mantra. We need to stay out of the fray because before we can have new creation, we have to have chaos. The Piscean age is that people who want to be in charge don't want to let go of where they're at, and so they are hanging on for dear life.

Did you know you had these intuitive gifts when you were younger?

No. It all opened up for me later in life. I had a friend who I spent time with when our children were in school together. She invited me to check out these herbs she was taking. She was going to Massachusetts to get connected with her herbal person, and through that there was a person who would work with you and dowse your energy. But at that point, he was using a muscle response. That's another part of dowsing. Anyway, he taught me how to do that at the time, and that started my curiosity. I got into using flower essences. Then, I had a health scare; I had ovarian cancer in the year 2000. A lot of things were just driving me to get more involved in the spiritual. Through my health and through different situations, I started dowsing, but I never thought that I would be able to dowse something like a labyrinth. I have many stories I could talk to you all day about. I belong to the American Dowsers Society in Vermont and that is one place where I go to dowsing meetings and so on. Dowsing is a skill, and we have a meeting in Falmouth once a month, that is spiritual. Dowsing is one portion of it, and the other is investigation into the paranormal, and we learn all kinds of interesting things there.

Back to numerology, Darlene said that the more you notice and know about numbers, the more that numbers will show up, as in the way I am always seeing the 11s and 22s.

You have a knowing of numbers that makes you pay attention and the more you learn about them the better you are going to be. Numbers are a universal language, and all people of all languages around the world understand and work with numbers. It's a good way to communicate. That's why Spirit likes using numbers.

My numerology reading with Darlene was more insightful than I expected, and an extremely powerful experience. Besides helping me see myself as unique and special, it also pointed to my potential, which is helpful to me, as I have been asking my guides for assistance with having more confidence in myself. Darlene used the letters from my full name, numbers from my birth date, and time of birth, to calculate a numerology blueprint. It was very in depth and comprehensive. She explained how my numbers indicated that I am a busy person with a lot to do in this life. That resonated with me, as I have always been very ambitious with projects and always find myself having too many activities going on at once. I always saw that as a negative trait, but the reading helped me see it as part of my specialness instead.

As with many of my readings in the making of this book, I was told this book project was one of the reasons I came into this life.

I believe everyone should have a numerology reading at some time in their life, and I highly recommend Darlene.

To contact Darlene for an appointment or more information, go to her website at www.darlenechadbourne.com.

Chapter 19

Laurie Lefebvre - Biodynamic Craniosacral Therapist
Yoga Instructor, Artist

A very unique and eclectic person, Laurie is gifted in traditional and nontraditional healing. She is a professional psychotherapist, energy worker, yoga instructor, and Biodynamic Craniosacral therapist. Having grown up in the Winslow Fairfield area, she is also an accomplished artist, and has been painting all her life. Laurie comes by her nontraditional healing gifts naturally. Her mother could do readings from a regular deck of playing cards, and her grandmother was a tea leaf reader.

Laurie had a near death experience when she was young, which she believes opened her up to her spiritual gifts. She is also a Reiki Shiham (teacher) and Shamanic Energy healer. Laurie learned about shamanism in Peru and has also studied yoga with a traditional yoga program and through Jaguar Path, a program that combines yoga and shamanism.

I met Laurie, who also goes by "La," at a holistic fair and I asked her if she could describe energetic cord cutting to me, as it was one of her offerings. La explained that it is a very powerful experience and suggested I should experience it first-hand if I was going to write about it. I learned that we all have emotional, energetic connections to the people in our lives, and sometimes it is necessary to sever energy cords if the connection is negative, or if that person is draining us of our energy. Cord cutting does not sever the love between people, just the negative attachment.

During my cord cutting session, La asked me to walk around in a small circle and think about the person whose negative energy cord I wanted to sever, and to repeat the words, "I release you, ___." Then, she asked me to stop and stand still as she used a beautiful brass Peruvian tool to cut (invisible energetic) strands away from my auric field in a very deliberate manner. It felt very powerful and emotional in that moment. After she finished the cutting, she used a feather to sweep up residual energy, followed by a rattle which she shook to break up remaining bits of energy. La assured me my tears were normal and were helpful in the process of letting go of the emotions associated with the negative energy. She said the energy she cleared was very heavy and clingy, and explained the cutting would open up space for different energy to move in. Interestingly, she also told me that soon I may hear from the person, because on some level, that person would sense a change. To be honest, I felt like I needed to go somewhere and have a good cry afterwards, and later I truly felt lighter. The memories of disagreements with this person, who is close to me, and the frequent thoughts about the negative feelings between us, no longer intruded on my thoughts.

As a healer, La sees and moves energy when working with a person, and she is able to get messages when working with the person's energy. She explained that we are all made up of energy, and that sometimes when she looks at a person's chakras, she is able to clear and eliminate imprints of energy on that person's energy field. La is able to see how specific issues such as relationships, or money issues, for example, have affected the person.

Some people get very light and energetic after a cord cutting, and some feel initially very sad letting go, and then peace or calmness, she added.

I asked La to describe herself and her gifts.

Words like medium or healer are all concepts. I see, feel, and move energy and then I get messages, because the energy often comes with messages. Chakra elimination, which works on imprints from past trauma on the body, is clearing the chakras. It involves a little more talk and focus about a specific issue that might be affecting a person's life over time. Some examples might be a person who has trouble with money, or someone who breaks bones in a patterned way, or a toxic relationship which has left a scar on the body.

I am a clear channel and work hard at keeping myself a "hollow bone" via being in nature, eating healthy, a vegan diet and doing my energy work, energy clearing and meditation. That is how I am able to see and know things about people's lives. I feel things, and I get information that way. People may call that a medium healing with energy work through the channel.

We are all made of energy. When I am in people's energy field, I see and feel what is there. I always ask to work with the highest vibration, the purest energy, the God, Christ, Holy Spirit, and then I can transmit the highest energies.

I am a therapist trained in the using Energy Movement Desensitizing Treatment; it's a proven modality to heal trauma. I can also use hypnosis to assist clients in coming up with their own understanding. Hypnosis is a useful tool in removing energy blocks.

We have attachments to people in our life and we are affected by their energy. Sometimes it is necessary to cut the negative kinds of things that affect the relationships between family members, a partner, or neighbor, and so on. When the energetic cords are severed, it frees up the person's energy. It clears space and makes them feel lighter. It can move some emotional stuff that a person might not realize is there, and it changes the pattern of whatever that was. A person can go back into the same patterning afterwards if they are not careful. When a cord cutting is done, the other person might feel something like a loss, and you might hear from them. Cord cutting is very powerful. We all interact in each other's energies.

Everyone is different. With some people I can feel dense energy, and sometimes I can see it. Sometimes it wraps itself around me a little bit. Once there was a really clingy energy cord that wrapped itself around a person, and when I tried to remove it, that cord started to go up my leg and I couldn't cut it off. I used a candle to burn it and my hair almost caught on fire. Every cord cutting is different. Some people have lots of emotions that are released even at the start of it, and with some people, their aura color changes. Everyone has had a different experience with it, and I will feel and see different things, too. I can see even very little attachments, and so I take my time to make sure that cord is gone.

A negative attachment can occur if you're in a relationship with someone and they cling to you too much or the other way around. If there was a negative influence and it took a lot of your energy, when you're cutting that off, you're feeling a loss like something is missing, and they associate that with you. Usually, people want to cut the cords from someone who sucked them dry, or another example could be a family member with a negative pattern of relationship. The person may feel the pulling away. The light energy never leaves us, just the heavy energy that is cut away. You can want to fall back into old patterns after the cord cutting if you are not mindful of it. It is important to keep a healthy balance.

Another way I work with people is as a Biodynamic Craniosacral Therapist. It is hands on, but it is not massage. We study the anatomy and physiology of the body, and we are constantly learning about all of the body systems and the blood and the brain and how the brain works with the body. It's pretty intense. It's an extension of the energy work I always was doing. I do Reiki, Energy work, Shamanism, and I still do that. It's all under the umbrella of working with the cosmic energy. It's body work, using your hands and touching the person on a deep level and in a deep way. Reiki is not as focused or specific. It is a training on how to be more in tune with the body's rhythms. Reiki does that too, but people who do Reiki are not as trained in the body mechanics, the physiology and the overall health of the bones, blood, organs and cerebral spinal fluid. There's a lot of science to it and it's very mystical too, because energy passes through the body. Anyone on the table can have a huge mystical experience. When I'm in there I allow the breath of life to do its work. With Biodynamic Craniosacral therapy, it's like working from the inside out, not the outside in. Biodynamic Craniosacral energy work comes from a lineage of osteopathy, and the osteopathy comes from Native Americans and the Native American healing. It's related to everything I do.

I love to paint in nature, and nature shows you on the outside what nature looks like inside the body. The trees and branches look like neurons in the brain, and the water, lakes, oceans, and rivers also reflect what you see inside the anatomy of the body. There are parts that look like jellyfish on the inside of the human body, and parts that look like animals and faces, and sometimes they look like flowers. For example, there are things in the immune system that look very floral and beautiful, and that's what you want to see because beautiful flora is protection from illness. Blood flows in tributaries like streams and rivers when you look at the body. When I look with my inner vision it shows me how it looks on the inside, with those kind of eyes. You are in that zone when doing that work on the body and you see the reflections of nature.

I don't heal people. I assist people in their own healing. People have to be in a space to find me, regardless of what I'm doing. My own energy system is so clear because I don't eat meat products. I don't drink, I don't smoke, or take any medicine. I'm a vegan and that helps when in the field. I am aware of my gifts; what I can and can't do, and energy that isn't mine passes through. I don't publicize my work very much. People come to me if they are meant to find me. That's how I see it.

To contact Laurie and for a list of all of her amazing offerings, go to https://laangelhealingarts.com.

Chapter 20

Susan St. Jean-Channel for the Council of Engma

I had a reading with Susan St. Jean many years ago, and I know her to be an extraordinary medium intuitive, but I recently learned that she offers so much more than just an accurate and healing personal reading. I am sure it may be difficult for some to absorb the information in this chapter.

In 2007, Susan St. Jean began to channel the Council of Engma, a compilation of spirits which include, Jesus, The Twelve Apostles, Archangel Michael, Archangel Raphael, Moses, Mohammed, and Einstein. This interview is but a mere sample of the sacred and profound teachings Susan has brought forth from the Council of Engma, and I highly recommend everyone to follow Susan's website, susanstjean-engma.com.

I was very moved by the interesting and deep conversation I had with Susan, and I was given a very deep and insightful personal message as well.

The following is an excerpt from our conversation:

For me, mediumship is not just about connecting with loved ones; it is about meeting up with people on their soul journey; not just the human aspect, but the soul aspect.

That is why we are here, as soul, and having a human experience, which is from what I've channeled from the Council of Engma, a part of the engine of creation. Therefore, I truly take that aspect of my path of service with a lot of reverence and focus. It's such an important part of my sessions with clients. I love mediumship and being able to tune in psychically, although I am very much against people taking what some reader said and making life decisions with it. That's not at all what my path of service is about. It is about empowering people to create the journey that they want and the future that they want. It is truly more about wanting to assist people so they don't have to come back. It is important that people are empowered, guided, and assisted to understand that they themselves are connected to Spirit, and to hone that remembrance, so that they develop their own connection and remembrance.

My teachers are not of this earth. For instance, years and years ago I took classes for Reiki 1 and Reiki 2 healing. The only reason that I did that was because it was a known word that was attached to energy work, versus just going up to someone and saying, "Would you like me to do energy work on you?"

At one point I went to a spiritualist church and took development classes for mediumship. It screwed me all up, because it got me all in my head, and I went from doing something that I naturally did, to intellectualizing, because I was 'learning' something. I only went for about a month, which was the best thing for my own soul's individual, energetic signature and planned trajectory.

Since then, everything has been unfolding for me in a very organic and soul aligned way. I have had incredible experiences over the years; ones that very few people know about, only those who have worked very closely with me and the Council of Engma. I am not about letters and credentials behind my name. I'm not even sure I know how I do what I do; it just happens. I am open and my highest prayer is that Mother-Father (God) always utilizes me in the highest vibrations of their love and light, to assist humanity, whether one individual at a time, or collectively or however it is that my soul is here to assist. I allow that intention and that desire to lead the way, and it works for me. Engma helps me understand that it is more of a deficit than advancement, to seek outside of yourself, pertaining to energy work. They have explained, "You are the modality. We all are the modality. There is no other way needed, for *you **are** the way as divine consciousness*, which **is** the modality that is utilized. It's not the human practitioner, it is Mother-Father. It is Source. It is the Creator utilized **as** you. Perceptually, **re-All-igning** yourselves with this truth and energetically re-merging in that consciousness of truth is the path to freedom and dissipation of all dis-ease and separation."

All humans have this capability and yet we aren't here to learn, we are here to remember. The more learning that we take on, for example about different belief systems, the more our experience is limited. Think about how many thousands of different religious systems there are, and yet it brings us further away from the one-ness. It is divisive instead of inclusive. From my perspective, and from what I have channeled from Engma, as human beings, we have to 'muck' it up. It is so simple, and yet because of our limiting human consciousness, we make it so much more complicated than it is.

I am not about being a fortune-telling psychic. Can I read people, of course, but that is not what I'm about. Again, I am about empowering people to not need a reader, **but instead** *reclaim the reader that they themselves are.*

Susan said that earlier in the conversation, when I admitted that I was not a professional writer, but 'just a town clerk' with a desire to gather information for this book, that Engma pointed out that is 'perfect'.

What Engma shared with me, is to step back from that self- judgment. There is no such thing as 'just a... town clerk.' Words are so important and powerful because we are such creative beings. We are creating in every moment. When you claim yourself as 'just a town clerk,' you are creating from a deficit point, or a lack, instead of embracing the powerful, Creator being that you are. All that is needed is to have your intention and desire to have anything that we do to be a loving, assisting consciousness, and then release it. For example, Engma always wanted me to be a blank chalkboard. They did not want me reading the Bible, or have strong beliefs about any specific religion. They wanted me blank because that is the best and easiest way to be a conduit of consciousness for Spirit and our soul to work with. It is because we are open. We are pliable.

There's nothing that they ever channel that has not energetically resonated with my own soul's truth. So, if I was in my human mind of a strong belief on any topic, I would not be an open conduit. Again, it goes back to how many letters someone acquires behind their name, because here in this dimension, in this human experience, the more letters, the better- so we think. Society says the more we have, the more we accomplish, then the more relevant and important we are. In fact, what it does is it thins out and stretches that divine thread that we just organically, innately are.

This is what they are saying and wanting to assist you with, Cathy, is that truly you don't need to be a writer, you just need to be an open conduit to be written through. I would really check in with your soul aspect and call forth your soul aspect to lead this venture. Try and set the human aspect aside, because the human aspect is Cathy saying, "I am not a professional writer, I am just a town clerk." That will be set aside so that there isn't that block. Just call forth what you are here to do. Align with why you are being led to do this, always from the highest best of all, and then just remain open. Don't try to figure it all out. Again, you will just get in there and get lost in the maze of your mind.

Engma also highlighted the word 'book' and replaced it with 'sharing' instead. That is your truth and yet you are out of alignment in word, and word is consciousness and vibration. Just ask Engma, your soul, or your guides and angels to assist you, so that you are aligning in your own consciousness, and in your own mind, when you're shooting yourself in the foot, or coming from a place of lack versus the powerful being that you are. Because there is no lack. It is part of the illusion of the human experience, but it is certainly not the reality of us as soul and as divine beings and creators. It is all Mother-Father (God). With everything from what I've channeled with Engma, there is only one self. One. That's where the oneness is. Everything in creation in equality, whether it is you, me, a dog, cat, raccoon, bird, or air, sun, or moon. It's all an expression of the one self.

I'll give you a teaching that Engma channeled years ago, and it's relevant to what we're speaking of. Imagine right now that you are God, and you have created Existence. In the beginning, there was only the 'is-ness,' just the is-ness of existence, which is the intelligence of love consciousness. So, much time goes by and it's beautiful and everything just 'is.' It just is. At some point, God got bored; very, very, very bored. God wanted to "be" that which God is and experience "Self." That's when Creation was birthed, through the Big Bang, which is the being-ness of God. The being-ness is everything in equality. A single blade of grass is God experiencing the one-self. A flower is God experiencing Self. It is an expression. It is what it's like to be the flower that I have created. I AM 'being' that. So, there was the is-ness, which is Source and then being-ness, which is Creator/Creation. Ultimately, at some point the whole experience of Existence will come full circle, back to the harmony of Love's one-ness within the being-ness. There is no duality in the is-ness of God. The duality we are experiencing here; hot and cold, right and wrong, male and female etc. is all part of the engine of evolution. Through the Natural Law of Free Will, the human ego manifests the judgment of duality. What is right, what is wrong, what is truth, or what isn't truth. All is the Soul/Source and Spirit/Creator experiencing Existence and All of the I AM is the engine of evolution. All is inclusively connected.

I admitted to Susan that this was all very hard for me to understand, and that before we talked, I read some of the information on her website and realized that I would have to read it over again more carefully when I had more time.

When I publish on my website what Engma has channeled, people often say, "Oh, I think I need to read this a few times to absorb it." Engma said in the very beginning that they purposely channel in a way that brings the human to inner stillness and contemplation, because that's where their God connection is. It is purposeful. It can be dense in the way that they channel, but whether the mind is absorbing it or not, you are getting the energetic transmission or download of the codes of that information as energy, because we are consciousness. We are not mind, we are not body, but we will be receiving that incoming awakening data energetically.

I told Susan it made me think of something I read on her website that when people hear ringing in their ears, it is because information is being downloaded. I told her I interestingly had three episodes of ringing in my ears before we spoke that afternoon.

The thing is that right now, Mother Earth, Mother Gaia, all of humanity, as physically dense beings, are receiving a lot of assistance from Source and our cosmic family. We are being infused with plasma energy and more, to assist in our ascension, and to assist in our remembrance. We are going from a three-dimensional reality into five-dimensional reality. We are evolving and getting a lot of assistance right now. People are experiencing a lot of emotional and physical challenges, which is good, because things are being brought up to the surface of awareness so they can be cleared and purged.

This is very interesting. A few years ago, a couple of friends wanted to go to Iceland, but my friend Sandy and I had absolutely no interest at all in going. We said, "Why would we want to go to Iceland, where it's so cold?" Then one day, I was in Florida walking on the beach with one of the friends who wanted to go, and Engma was channeling a lot of information. Right in the middle of the channeling they interrupted themselves and said, "We need you to go to Iceland." I looked at my friend and said, "Oh, I guess I am going to Iceland! They are telling me we need to go because we have to seed the Divine Feminine Energy into the Aurora Borealis."

That night they (Engma) told me that my friend Sandy, who works with Engma and me, also needed to go, and it was mid-March when we went. Interestingly, just today, a half hour before I talked with you, Engma suddenly led my eyes to a video on the side of my computer screen. The article said that for the first time in over nine hundred years, a volcano had just erupted in Iceland, just outside of the same town we were in. It was where we had seeded the Divine Feminine into the Aurora Borealis. Again, it is about always being open, and honoring what's being asked of you, when you're being guided and directed. It's not knowing what it's going to be about in the big picture, but just having presence and action of what is being asked of you.

We were asked to seed the Divine Feminine energy into the Aurora Borealis on March 17th. That night it was pitch black out and we couldn't see the Aurora Borealis, but Engma guided us exactly where to go and then guided us through a detailed step by step ceremony to seed the Divine Feminine. It was freezing out and after we did this, I went to open the door to get in the vehicle and Engma said, "Look up! Look up!" I looked up and there was the Aurora Borealis! In hindsight thinking about it, that is the only way we would have known that we were successful. If it had been visible the whole time, how would we have known if we were successful or not?

I had never heard of the Divine Feminine energy being seeded into the Aurora Borealis before, and I asked Susan what this was all about.

A couple of months before this happened, Engma started channeling about Mother Earth and about the Divine Feminine. I didn't know anything about any of it. Once again, I was just going where I was being lead, and they had us do a bunch of work for a couple months with Mother Earth, specifically within Mother Earth: the lay lines of Mother Earth, the grid system, and the crystalline grid system. We did a lot of work activating that energy within Mother Earth. They explained the grids were like the veins of Mother Earth, and that they were all clogged with the density of masculine energy. So, as directed, for a few months we worked on clearing it by merging with rock consciousness, crystal consciousness, tree consciousness, and with the root systems that ground into Mother Earth. It was a whole big, elaborate experience of doing the ground work, literally, and also connecting the crystalline grid within Mother Gaia, with the Christ Consciousness grid that surrounds Mother Earth. That as well was all part of the needed preparation to seed the Divine Feminine. Again, All inclusively merged in the reality of Divine Oneness assisting the One Self.

I found out today, that just a few days ago the volcano that erupted in Iceland was right outside of Reykjavik. And literally, we were in the town of Reykjavik, and we were told it had to be on March 17th, which is a very significant number for Engma, and that is had to be at 2:17 a.m. I don't know where exactly we drove to, but we were instructed to go to the outskirts of Reykjavik. All I know is that this volcano was on the outside of Reykjavik, and that is where we seeded the Divine Feminine. I haven't received any more information as far as our connection with it all, but it is interesting that in the last couple years, and especially now, the ascension process that I talk about on my website, is all about the world needing the energy of the Divine Feminine now for balance. It is all coming full circle.

It is all about being open in my heart and in my soul in purity wanting to assist, and that, I feel, is the best advice I could ever give you or anyone. Forget credentials. When it comes to serving spiritually, the only credentials any of us need are that we are the expression of Mother-Father (God). What more credentials could you need?

It's not about doing. It's about being; just simply being the being-ness from Source's is-ness that we are. It's the doing-ness of more, more, more, that distracts and mucks everything up, really, when you think about it in the big picture. The smarter you are, the more degrees you have, the more successful you are, and the more money you make, is not why we are here. As part of Creator's being-ness, Humanity is here to evolve as soul/source intelligence through being and experiencing love consciousness. We are not here to only accumulate material things and riches, even though that is also the breath of free will within all possibility of being-ness. Yet, without the breath of love's is-ness, experiencing all the wealth and material things becomes breathless, empty and lifeless from the wholeness of existence.

I told Susan that I understood that because what I truly want the most is time to enjoy our camp at Moosehead Lake. Being able to someday spend the whole summer at camp is my dream.

May I offer you something? The important thing I want to share is that you are not about material things, and yet they (Engma) did highlight that you said you wanted to just be at camp and enjoy. They said that you can do that anytime you want to, because you are not just a physical body. You don't have to go there physically; you can just 'be' there. Again, this is part of the mucking things up that we humans do because we are in such a limitation of consciousness. You may be thinking that there's too much snow on the ground right now so you can't go to camp, however you can bi-locate and have it be a beautiful, sunny summer day. Just create it and experience that.

Oh, so you mean we just need to find the joy wherever we imagine it to be?

We are the joy, so conversely, we simply need to imagine where we joy-fully want to be **as** joy in our unlimited truth as consciousness. We as humans seek out what will make us happy. The truth is, happiness is already there, and we just need to plug into it. Picture a big, thick extension cord and you have the plug in your hand. Humans have it plugged into all the wrong things through our perceptual lens and focus. We have it plugged into the lack of, versus what really is. It's just a matter of unplugging and then plugging into the love and joy that we are. All of humanity's truth is that we are **experiencing** being human, and during this experience of beingness, we forget that we are part of the engine of creational evolution. However, that doesn't mean with intentional, perceptual focus, we can't claim back our origin's truth of seeded beingness from the nucleus of the first breath of ALL that is in existence. We are here experiencing human-beingness to breathe the breath of evolution more so through our own existential truth's rebirth in our human consciousness.

I'm being told that this is not at all what you thought this (interview) was going to be. (Laughter.)

I told Susan I had a list of things to ask, but I was intimidated by the fact that the Council of Engma includes Jesus Himself, and the Twelve Apostles, Archangel Michael, Archangel Rafael, Mohammed and Moses and the even Einstein which is just so incredible that I was hoping she would just share information as she had been.

Jesus just crossed out his name 'Jesus' to show you that you are acknowledging everyone, but you are putting one before the other. The relevance of Jesus has no more relevance than any other; that is basically what He is saying. That is what creates separation. Jesus is more of a being in a consciousness of, like you are my brother, you are my sister, in equality, inclusively. It is not about structures or stained-glass windows. In fact, just literally this morning something else popped up on my computer out of nowhere. It was a document about a channeling from the Council of Engma about the burning of the Notre Dame Cathedral, which I had forgotten about and never finished. It was pretty intense. It was about how the burning of Notre Dame was actually a blessing, and it was Jesus speaking about it saying that it was just a building, or structure of teaching that was misrepresentative of his teachings. The religion was built from an aspect of free will of being-ness that was not holy, not inclusive in love's wholeness. It was for more lower, denser, egoic vibrating reasons, and because of humanity's overall evolution vibrationally, anything of untruth can no longer last. It must give way and transcend because it cannot be contained any longer. No one needs a structure because you are the temple. We ourselves are the temple, from the is-ness and being-ness that we are.

Interestingly, they just highlighted another thing. Years back they had a teaching on the consciousness of the word 'healing' that we use as humans. If I am an energy practitioner, or if I am a client, and it is my perception in consciousness that I 'need' or that I am 'giving' a healing, then I am coming from a place of perceptual lack as Consciousness. Humanity is doing it and getting it all wrong. Just by the verbiage which is energy. It is consciousness. For example, to say, "I have a client at 3 o'clock that needs a healing," needs a healing, I am sanctifying that they are not the powerful being that they are, and that they are in need. What they explained is that, that in itself is what needs to be healed. It is the perception of the belief and where the focus point is. If the focus point is, I need a healing, I am in a deficit. Then that consciousness is where I am manifesting from. It's how I am creating, and I am creating from a lack. I said to them, "What do we call it?" They said, 'energy work.' In other words, energy might need assistance to raise, shift, or move, but it's not because of a lack.

They (Engma) are going back to the credentials of all the different healing modalities. It's all so unnecessary because what it is doing, is it is anchoring in the consciousness of lack. The more healers and the more ways of healing that are being put upon humanity's consciousness, are kinking the hose more and more from our own divinity, and the powerful Creator beings that we are. It is rampant everywhere in our consciousness because it is embedded in our foundation of human consciousness. It is important to know that we are in an un-doing time. We need to undo, so that the new can be raised. But we must undo that which we have been feeding ourselves, which is of so many untruths that are the nutrients with which we are feeding our consciousness.

Our words come from our thoughts. However, no one can change anything unless we are aware. Call forth your soul, guides and angels to highlight your thoughts of lack. Invite them into your vibration and ask them to assist you with your perceptual awareness. Whether it's Engma or a spirit guide or a loved one, they are limited with the level of assistance they can give us until we, with our free will, give them the okay. We need to give them permission.

That is the nutrient with which you are feeding your consciousness. One of the chapters that they want in my upcoming book is called the "Nutrients of Consciousness," because that is really what we feed ourselves, the nutrients of consciousness. Because we are here having this physical experience, we think of nutrients as food, yet the nutrients of consciousness that we feed ourselves, are so much more important.

I admitted to Susan that it is hard to conceive that Jesus, and Engma, are actually able to respond to my questions and talk directly to me.

After a long pause, Susan said Jesus said, "Why not you?"

Susan told me about an ordeal from an illness she has just endured and said that it was a transformative time which she would not want to re-live, but she is grateful for.

I did the work. A lot of the experiences that happened triggered some things that I thought I had worked through already. That's the gift, you know, that if someone were to experience something that triggers us, it brings it up to the surface, to our awareness of something that needs to be worked through, purged and released. You know, interestingly, they channeled something about two years ago, and what they communicated has some very strong symbolism, but it gets the point across. They said that humans are like men, you always pull out just in time to not impregnate. They went on to explain that we don't want to feel the pain, so we drink, we drug, we shop too much, and we watch too much television. We do anything to numb the experience, and before we feel the pain, we pull out.

They explained that in order to purge anything that we experience, we have to fully impregnate ourselves with it. We have to go to that pain. So instead of the desire and the prayer to please take this away, we should be rolling up our sleeves and saying, "Mother-Father, bring me to the pain." It is not the natural thing to do. Yet we, as souls, chose everything that we have experienced and will continue to experience for the soul's evolution.

When we die, we shed our body because there is no such thing as death. Think of it. When someone says for example, "My loved one has just died." We are anchoring an untruth, more and more in the consciousness, not just of ourselves, not of our family, but of humanity as a collective. There is no such thing as death. We literally just shed the vehicle. The body is no different than the four tires on the vehicle that we drive around in. It is just a vehicle that our soul uses to traverse this plane of existence. That's all it is. The body dies, but the soul does not die.

Think of how much more a loved one can experience without a body. Think of Cathy bi-locating to her camp. They can be with us all of the time in ways that they couldn't when they were in the physical body. Their own omni-presence can be at your wedding and your brother's wedding and someone else's funeral all at the same time, without the body. We think of it as, like Engma explained eons ago, "we have it all backwards." What we as humans call birth is actually more of the death. What we call the death is actually more of the birth. We are re-birthing back. When we go into our physical body, we forget our truth as divine beings. There is a death in that, because we as humans forget how powerful we are. We are not just a town clerk in Wayne, Maine. That is the death.

My advice is to stay in a heart centered place of pure aligned intention, of being aligned to be the loving light we are, and being available to assist in Creator's evolution.

I am being told to tell you that "You've got this!" Followed up with, "Just make sure of what the 'this' is, first and foremost."

Susan stepped aside to let The Council of Engma channel.

Afterwards, I summarized my message from Engma to Susan, (who doesn't remember when she goes into channeling), that I was told to halt the interviews for now, take a hiatus and go within and interview myself, (do an inner-view) and to just 'be'…and then when I continue with the interviews, the process will be like the ease of skiing down a hill on my skis. Also in closing, Engma said to me, "You are blessed. This journey is being blessed. Don't do the journey; be the journey. Just be. In my Father's love, we remain with you. Call upon us as you wish. We and others are here. Enjoy the you, as Cathy, that you are. In-joy. Do not seek the 'en'-joy, simply be the in (joy). All is well."

I was deeply honored to talk with Susan and to have received the very personal, powerful, and loving message from the Council of Engma.

For more information about Susan and the Council of Engma, please go to her website at susanstjean-engma.com

Why is it trees understand they have to be free-flowing and bend
a little with the wind to unify in their Oneness as a forest,

yet, we as human beings allow our egos to keep us petrified in a
separate stance as a society?

To perceive something as one way or right is not always wise nor
what will lead you to understand truth and love.

Wouldn't it be a loving world if we could lay our swords of ego
down at the same time to allow the materialization of our Soul's
Divine Gracious Harmonization?

Thank you for being a person whose spirit stands tall among the
trees displaying Mother-Father's beautiful visions of a loving
world!

©2000SusanSt.Jean

About the Author

Cathy Cook lives in Wayne, Maine with her husband Rick, where she works as the Town Clerk and is a Co-President of the Wayne Historical Society.

An outdoors enthusiast, Cathy is also passionate about the spirit world which has always been fascinating to her. During the process of interviewing gifted people for this book, she has been propelled forward in her own spiritual growth. The higher perspective on life Cathy has gained in the process of the making of this book, and the tools she learned, have enhanced her life experience.

Cathy has met many wonderful people collecting these stories; many of whom she was meant to meet. She hopes to open minds to the spirit world which she fervently believes in.

Copies of Cathy's other books may be purchased online from Amazon Books.

Hauntings from Wayne and Beyond

Hauntings from Wayne and Beyond 2

Hauntings from Eastport and Beyond

You may contact Cathy by email: cookcathy971@gmail.com

www.ingramcontent.com/pod-product-compliance
Lightning Source LLC
Chambersburg PA
CBHW060542160726
47991CB00001B/423